GREENHOUSE

GARDENING

FOR BEGINNERS

D1713631

Master the Art of Efficient Plant Growth in Any Climate, Elevating Your Home Gardening to New Heights

Haley Sherwood

TABLE OF CONTENTS

CHAPTER 1: INTRODUCTION TO GREENHOUSE GARDENING

1.1. WHAT IS GREENHOUSE GARDENING?

Greenhouse gardening is a practical approach to cultivating a diverse range of plants in a controlled environment, independent of external weather conditions. This method utilizes enclosed structures, which can range from basic frames covered with clear plastic to sophisticated glass or polycarbonate greenhouses equipped with technology for climate control.

Originating in the 16th century with the European orangeries designed to protect citrus trees from frost, the concept of the greenhouse has evolved significantly. Initially a luxury for the affluent, today's greenhouses are tools of efficiency and sustainability, accessible to gardeners at all levels.

The principle behind greenhouse gardening lies in its ability to regulate the internal climate—capturing solar energy to create a stable temperature and accommodating various plants' needs across different seasons. For example, plants that thrive in warmer climates, such as tomatoes, can grow alongside cooler-temperature plants like kale, all under the same roof.

A well-managed greenhouse not only optimizes plant health and yield but also contributes to ecological sustainability. By growing your own vegetables, fruits, and herbs, you reduce your dependence on store-bought produce, which often involves extensive packaging and long-distance transportation, contributing to carbon emissions and waste.

Effective greenhouse gardening requires understanding and managing several variables: the transparency of the walls for maximum sunlight exposure, the insulation to retain heat, and systems to control ventilation, heating, and humidity. Each factor plays a critical role in creating the ideal conditions for plant growth.

Aside from its practical benefits, greenhouse gardening offers a tranquil refuge from the hectic pace of modern life. It provides a unique opportunity to connect with nature, promoting mental well-being and a sense of accomplishment from nurturing plants from seed to harvest.

However, embarking on greenhouse gardening involves initial challenges, including costs and the selection of appropriate technology and materials. It's crucial to approach these obstacles with thorough research and planning, considering your specific gardening goals and the particular needs of the plants you wish to grow.

Ultimately, the success of a greenhouse garden depends less on its size and more on the quality of care it receives. Whether your greenhouse is modest or expansive, the key to productivity lies in consistent and attentive gardening practices. By integrating thoughtful planning with careful execution, greenhouse gardening can be a rewarding endeavor that enhances not only your dining table but also your community and the environment.

1.2. BENEFITS OF GROWING IN A GREENHOUSE

Choosing to set up a greenhouse can revolutionize your gardening by offering a range of practical benefits that enhance both plant growth and your gardening experience. Here's a straightforward look at what you gain from investing in a greenhouse:

Extended Growing Season: One of the primary advantages of a greenhouse is the ability to extend the growing season. Inside the controlled environment of a greenhouse, temperature and weather conditions are regulated, allowing for earlier planting in the spring and extended growing into the colder months. This means you can enjoy fresh produce like crisp lettuce or ripe tomatoes far beyond their usual outdoor growing season.

Cultivation of Exotic Plants: With a greenhouse, you're not limited to local plant varieties. The stable conditions inside allow you to explore growing exotic or tropical plants that would not survive the colder temperatures of your local climate. Whether it's citrus trees or rare flowers, a greenhouse opens up a whole new world of gardening possibilities.

Consistent and Reliable Harvests: Weather can be unpredictable and often detrimental to plant growth. A greenhouse protects your plants from the extremes of weather such as frost, heavy rains, and high winds. This protection leads to more reliable yields since your plants are less likely to be damaged by weather conditions.

Protection from Pests and Predators: A greenhouse provides a barrier against pests and wildlife that could harm your plants. While not impervious, the controlled access makes it easier to manage any infestations and significantly reduces the likelihood of pests and diseases.

Efficient Use of Resources: Water conservation is another significant benefit. In a greenhouse, you can collect and recycle water, and the enclosed space reduces water loss through evaporation. Additionally, heating and cooling can be managed more efficiently in a greenhouse than in an open garden, potentially leading to energy savings if you use renewable energy sources.

Gardening in Any Climate: A greenhouse essentially neutralizes the external climate. This means you can create a suitable growing environment regardless of whether you live in a very cold or very hot area. It allows gardeners in unfavorable climates to grow a wider variety of plants year-round.

Higher Quality and Healthier Plants: Plants grown in a greenhouse typically exhibit better health and quality. The controlled environment allows you to optimize conditions for growth, leading to healthier plants that can produce more robust and aesthetically pleasing fruits and flowers.

Learning and Experimentation: Owning a greenhouse offers a unique opportunity to experiment with plant growing conditions and learn more about botany and gardening techniques. It's a hands-on way to engage with your hobby and continually improve your skills.

Enhanced Well-being: Beyond the tangible benefits, spending time in a greenhouse can be incredibly therapeutic. The peaceful environment helps reduce stress and promote a sense of well-being. Gardening in a greenhouse can become a meditative activity that helps you reconnect with nature.

In essence, a greenhouse can transform your gardening experience by providing you with the tools to produce a variety of plants more effectively and with greater satisfaction. Whether you're a novice looking to get started or an experienced gardener aiming to expand your capabilities, a greenhouse offers valuable advantages that extend well beyond the basic cultivation of plants.

Community and Connection

The benefits transcend the individual, radiating outward to infuse the community. A greenhouse becomes a node of connection, a shared interest sparking dialogues, encouraging seed swaps, and engendering bonds fortified by the love of growth. Its bounty spills into kitchens and dining tables, not just within your home but extends to neighbors, friends, and local food banks—the seedlings of a deeply rooted community where care multiplies.

In essence, the greenhouse is not merely a method for agricultural yield but a catalyst for a vibrant lifestyle. The nurturing dome incites a symphony of benefits that ripple through your health, the community, and on a grander scale, the environment. Its existence is a testament to the harmony achievable between human ingenuity and nature's bounty, a balance where both flourish. As we tend to our plants under the sheltering panels, we are not just growers of greens—we are cultivators of life, curators of nature, and stewards of a sustainable future.

Choosing the right type of greenhouse is like picking a home where your plants can thrive under your care, shielded from external elements. Different greenhouses suit different needs, depending on your space, climate, and style preferences.

Traditional Free-Standing Greenhouses: These standalone structures are popular for their versatility and full sun exposure, making them ideal for a variety of plants. With a classic pitched roof, they shed rain and snow easily and can be placed strategically to optimize light throughout the year.

Attached or Lean-To Greenhouses: Attached to a building, these greenhouses are great for small spaces or for gardeners wanting close access to their plants. The shared wall helps retain heat, reducing heating costs, though it may limit sunlight exposure.

A-Frame Greenhouses: Known for their triangular shape, A-Frame greenhouses are effective in snowy areas as their design prevents snow accumulation. They are simpler to construct and provide good air circulation, helping prevent plant diseases.

Dome Greenhouses: These round, geometric structures are not only visually striking but also highly durable and efficient at distributing light and facilitating air flow. Their unique shape makes them resistant to wind and harsh weather.

Cold Frames and Hotbeds: Smaller than other greenhouses, cold frames and hotbeds are perfect for starting seedlings or extending the growing season. Hotbeds include a heat source, giving plants a warm start in early spring or extra warmth during colder months.

Materials and Construction

Wood: Provides a classic look and can be painted or stained, but requires maintenance to prevent decay, especially in humid conditions.

Aluminum: Durable, rust-resistant, and requires little maintenance, making it a more costly upfront investment but economical over time.

Galvanized Steel: Offers excellent strength and durability, ideal for regions with heavy snow or strong winds.

PVC: Lightweight and inexpensive, it's a good choice for temporary or seasonal use but has a shorter lifespan than metal frames.

Cladding Options

Glass: Offers excellent light transmission and longevity but is fragile and can be expensive.

Polycarbonate: Provides good insulation and protects plants from direct sunlight, reducing the risk of burns. It's durable and less likely to break than glass.

Polyethylene Film: An economical choice for beginners or temporary structures, easy to replace but less durable than other materials.

Fiberglass: Durable and diffuses light well, but may yellow over time.

Additional Considerations

Ventilation: Essential for temperature and humidity control, options include roof vents, side vents, and automated systems.

Access and Layout: Doors should provide easy access and aid ventilation. Inside, shelves and benches should maximize space and support plant growth efficiently.

Choosing the right greenhouse involves balancing your gardening goals with practical considerations like budget, climate, and space. Each type offers unique benefits, allowing you to create a tailored growing environment for a diverse array of plants. By understanding these options, you can make an informed decision that best suits your gardening needs and aspirations, setting the stage for a productive and enjoyable greenhouse gardening experience.

CHAPTER 2: PLANNING YOUR GREENHOUSE

2.1. CHOOSING THE RIGHT LOCATION

Selecting the right location for your greenhouse is crucial for the success of your gardening endeavors. Here's how to ensure that your plants thrive in their new environment.

Sunlight: The most important factor is ensuring your greenhouse receives enough sunlight. Aim for a south-facing position in the northern hemisphere to maximize exposure during all seasons. It's critical that the winter sun, which has a lower angle, can reach your plants, so keep this path clear of any obstructions.

Shade and Overexposure: While sunlight is essential, too much direct exposure during the summer can be harmful. Utilize natural shade from deciduous trees, which provide leafy coverage in the summer and drop their leaves in the winter, ensuring a seasonal balance.

Wind Protection: Protecting your greenhouse from strong winds is vital, as they can cool your greenhouse rapidly. Use natural barriers like fences or building walls that do not cast shade on your greenhouse but can effectively block the wind.

Drainage: Proper drainage is essential to prevent water accumulation around your greenhouse. Choose a location with natural slope or consider elevating the structure slightly to facilitate water runoff.

Accessibility: Place your greenhouse close enough to your home to make regular visits convenient, even in bad weather. Ensure the path is clear and can accommodate garden tools and wheelbarrows.

Resource Proximity: Consider the proximity to water and electricity sources, especially if you plan to install heating systems or automated watering systems in the greenhouse. This can significantly reduce installation costs and daily hassle.

Neighborhood Considerations: Be mindful of the impact of your greenhouse on your neighbors. Avoid blocking their views or casting shadows on their property. Also, check local zoning regulations to understand what structures are permitted.

Pest Management: Keep your greenhouse away from areas prone to wild pests and diseases, such as wooded areas or unkempt fields. This reduces the risk of pest infestations that could damage your plants.

Aesthetics: Your greenhouse should not only be functional but also integrate aesthetically with your property. Place it where it can be seen from your home, making it a pleasing part of your view and daily life.

When planning the location of your greenhouse, visualize the daily movement of the sun and seasonal changes. This foresight will help you optimize the placement for light exposure, protection, and functionality, setting the stage for a successful greenhouse gardening experience. By considering these practical aspects, you create not just a space for growing plants, but a sanctuary where both you and your garden can prosper.

2.2. Sizing and Design Considerations

When planning your greenhouse, sizing and design are critical factors that determine how well your space functions and meets your gardening goals. Here's how to make the best choices for your gardening needs.

Determining Size: Start with the types of plants you want to grow, considering their mature sizes and space requirements. Think about your gardening approach—whether you prefer densely packed shelves or larger beds of soil. Also, incorporate pathways for easy access and movement inside the greenhouse. If you're limited by outdoor space, consider vertical solutions like tall shelving or hanging plants to maximize your growing area.

Choosing a Design: Your greenhouse should be a blend of functionality and personal style. Materials like glass provide clear viewing and excellent light penetration, while polycarbonate panels might offer better insulation and durability. Consider the structure's framework too—metal gives a modern look, while wood offers a traditional feel.

Orientation: A south-facing orientation is generally best in the northern hemisphere to capture maximum sunlight during winter. However, in warmer climates, an east-west orientation can help manage heat by minimizing direct sun in the afternoons.

Architectural Style: The design of your greenhouse should complement its function. Lean-to greenhouses are great for space-saving and can utilize an existing wall for additional heat retention. Freestanding greenhouses offer more light exposure and can be placed in optimal locations for sun and protection. Dome-shaped greenhouses are efficient at resisting wind and distributing light evenly.

Climate Control: Consider how the size and design of your greenhouse will affect its internal climate. Larger greenhouses may require more heating, while compact designs need good air circulation to prevent damp conditions. Plan for climate control systems like heaters, fans, and vents to maintain a stable environment throughout the year.

Future Flexibility: Design your greenhouse to be adaptable as your gardening interests and expertise grow. Features like adjustable shelving or modular design can accommodate changes in the types of plants you grow or allow for the introduction of new technologies like hydroponics.

Material Selection: Choose durable materials that balance cost, maintenance, and performance. Galvanized steel frames are robust and long-lasting, while wood frames offer aesthetic appeal but may require more upkeep. For glazing, consider materials like double-walled polycarbonate for excellent insulation and light diffusion, which helps prevent plant burn.

Integration with the Environment: Design your greenhouse to harmonize with its surroundings. Place it to optimize light exposure, protect from extreme weather, and complement your home's aesthetics. Consider environmental sustainability in your design, such as incorporating rainwater harvesting or using recycled materials.

Budget Considerations: Define your budget early in the planning process. Consider phased building or expandable designs if upfront costs are a concern. Investing in high-quality foundational elements can save money long term by reducing the need for frequent repairs or upgrades.

By thoroughly considering each of these elements, you can create a greenhouse that not only meets your immediate needs but also adapts to future ambitions. This careful planning ensures that your greenhouse is a productive, enjoyable space for years to come.

Creating a greenhouse involves careful financial planning to ensure that your gardening dreams don't become a financial burden. Here's how to effectively budget for both the setup and ongoing costs of your greenhouse.

Start-Up Costs

1. **Greenhouse Structure**: The cost varies significantly depending on size, materials, and whether you opt for a DIY project or a pre-fabricated kit. Prices can range from a few hundred dollars for a basic model to several thousand for a large, durable structure.

2. **Foundation and Flooring**: A solid foundation is crucial for the stability of your greenhouse. Costs will depend on the materials (e.g., concrete, wood) and the size of your greenhouse. Flooring options like gravel or concrete also vary in price.

3. **Utilities Installation**: If your greenhouse needs electricity and water, the installation costs will depend on the proximity to existing utility lines. Adding gas for heating might be necessary, depending on your climate.

4. **Environmental Control Systems**: Basic ventilation might be inexpensive, but automated systems for temperature and humidity control can increase your initial investment.

5. **Shelving and Planting Surfaces**: Costs depend on the materials used and whether you purchase ready-made units or build your own. Consider the weight and maintenance requirements of different materials.

6. **Tools and Equipment**: Basic gardening tools may not cost much, but specialized equipment like automated watering systems or grow lights will add to your start-up costs.

Operational Expenses

1. **Heating and Cooling**: The energy costs for heating and cooling your greenhouse can vary widely based on your climate and the efficiency of your systems.

2. **Watering and Irrigation**: Manual watering is inexpensive, but an automated system might increase your water bills. Collecting rainwater can help reduce these costs.

3. **Supplies**: Regular purchases of soil, fertilizers, and other consumables can add up. Opting for high-quality, sustainable products can offer better long-term value.

4. **Maintenance and Repairs**: Set aside funds for maintaining and repairing your greenhouse. This includes replacing broken panels, fixing leaks, and upgrading outdated systems.

5. **Pest Control and Disease Management**: Investing in organic and sustainable pest management solutions can help maintain the health of your plants and reduce the need for expensive chemical treatments.

Balancing Quality with Cost

Investing in better quality materials and equipment can save money in the long run by reducing the need for frequent replacements and repairs. However, it's important to balance this with your immediate budget constraints.

Using Repurposed Materials

Consider using repurposed or second-hand materials to save money. This can include anything from reclaimed wood for structural elements to used containers for planters.

Planning for Unexpected Costs

Always include a contingency budget of around 10-20% of your total expected costs to cover unexpected expenses. This can help manage unforeseen costs without straining your finances.

Financing Options

If necessary, explore financing options such as personal loans, grants, or community funding initiatives. Some regions offer financial support for agricultural or educational projects, which could apply to your greenhouse.

Budgeting Summary

- Estimate all start-up costs including the structure, foundation, utilities, control systems, shelving, and equipment.

- Factor in ongoing costs like energy, water, supplies, maintenance, and pest control.

- Invest in quality where it counts, but use repurposed materials to cut costs.

- Prepare for unexpected expenses with a contingency fund.

- Consider various financing options if upfront cash is not available.

A well-planned budget is key to ensuring that your greenhouse is both a productive garden space and a financially sustainable project.

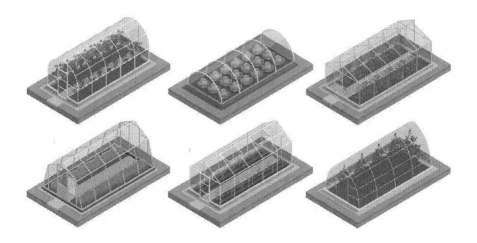

3.1. COLD FRAMES AND STARTER GREENHOUSES

Cold frames and starter greenhouses represent an essential stepping stone for aspiring greenhouse gardeners, offering a manageable and economical entry into more extensive horticultural projects. These smaller, simpler structures are perfect for beginners and provide numerous learning opportunities without the overwhelming complexity and cost of larger greenhouses.

Cold Frames: Cold frames are basic structures that function almost like miniature greenhouses. Typically constructed low to the ground, they consist of a transparent lid made of glass or clear plastic, which allows sunlight to enter while retaining heat to protect plants from cold weather. Cold frames are particularly useful for extending the growing season by sheltering young seedlings from frost, helping root cuttings in early spring, or even allowing the cultivation of cold-tolerant vegetables into the winter months.

The simplicity of cold frames also lends itself to versatility in materials and design. Whether you build one from scratch using spare wood and old windows or assemble a kit, cold frames are a low-cost, effective solution for early and late-season gardening challenges. They teach important lessons in temperature management, light control, and moisture maintenance, all within a compact space that's easy to manage.

Starter Greenhouses: For those ready to graduate from cold frames but not quite prepared for a large, permanent greenhouse, starter greenhouses are an ideal middle step. These are typically small enough to fit comfortably in a backyard but large enough to walk into and work inside, providing more space for a greater variety of plants and more sophisticated environmental control systems than cold frames.

Starter greenhouses allow gardeners to experiment with a wider array of horticultural techniques and plant species, from delicate flowers to hearty vegetables. They also offer the ability to control the environment more precisely, with options for installing basic heating and cooling systems, thus extending the growing potential even further.

The design and setup of a starter greenhouse can be as straightforward or as involved as your skills and budget allow. Many models come with shelving and hanging systems to maximize space and can be equipped with automated irrigation and climate control systems as your comfort with greenhouse gardening grows.

Both cold frames and starter greenhouses serve not only as protection for plants but also as invaluable learning tools. They provide hands-on experience with the fundamentals of greenhouse gardening, such as understanding the microclimate within your structure, learning how to optimize conditions based on seasonal changes, and managing the delicate balance between humidity, temperature, and ventilation.

These structures encourage experimentation and gradual expansion into more complex gardening projects. They are also significantly more affordable and less demanding in terms of maintenance and resource consumption compared to larger greenhouses, making them a smart choice for beginners.

In essence, starting with a cold frame or a small greenhouse allows you to build confidence and expertise as you prepare for potentially larger and more intricate gardening projects. They are excellent for mastering the basics of plant care and environmental management, setting a strong foundation for a rewarding journey into the world of greenhouse gardening.

3.2. TUNNEL GREENHOUSES AND HOOP HOUSES

Tunnel greenhouses and hoop houses represent an ideal blend of functionality and cost-effectiveness, making them excellent choices for both novice and experienced gardeners. These structures are defined by their arching frames, typically made of metal or plastic, which are then covered with a durable, transparent plastic. This design not only maximizes sunlight exposure but also creates an efficient microclimate conducive to plant growth.

Advantages of Tunnel Greenhouses and Hoop Houses:

1. **Affordability**: One of the biggest draws of these structures is their relatively low cost compared to more permanent greenhouse constructions. The materials needed are minimal, and the design is simple enough for DIY assembly, reducing initial investment significantly.

2. **Flexibility**: These greenhouses can be easily expanded or reconfigured as your gardening needs change. The modular nature of their design allows for extensions to be added as needed without extensive modifications.

3. **Season Extension**: By trapping heat and protecting plants from external weather conditions, these greenhouses enable gardeners to start their growing seasons earlier and extend them later into the fall and even winter, depending on the climate.

4. **Simplicity of Use**: The straightforward design of tunnel greenhouses and hoop houses makes them easy to use and maintain. They can be ventilated by simply rolling up the sides, and various covering materials can be used to suit different weather conditions and planting needs.

Design Considerations:

- **Materials**: Choosing the right materials for your hoops and covers is crucial. Galvanized steel or durable PVC pipes are popular choices for the frame, offering both strength and resistance to weather. The plastic sheeting should be UV-resistant to prevent degradation by sunlight and sturdy enough to withstand wind and snow.

- **Size and Shape**: The height and width of the tunnel will determine what types of plants can be successfully grown. Taller tunnels accommodate larger plants like tomatoes and cucumbers, while lower designs are suitable for salads and herbs. The shape of the arch can also impact light penetration and air circulation, factors essential for plant health.

- **Climate Control**: Managing the internal climate is key. While passive solar heat accumulation is beneficial, overheating can become an issue. Incorporating adjustable side vents or peak vents can help regulate temperatures. For colder climates, supplemental heating might be necessary to maintain optimal growing conditions.

- **Irrigation**: Efficient watering systems are vital. Drip irrigation is a popular choice for these structures as it delivers water directly to plant roots, minimizing waste and preventing the spread of disease through splashing.

- **Pest and Disease Management**: The enclosed environment can protect plants from many pests and diseases, but it can also create conditions that some pests favor. Regular monitoring and the introduction of beneficial insects or organic pest control methods can help manage these risks.

Using Your Tunnel Greenhouse or Hoop House:

Utilizing these structures effectively involves careful planning and management. They are excellent for growing a wide range of crops, from leafy greens and herbs to more heat-loving vegetables like peppers and eggplants. Experimentation with plant spacing, trellising, and vertical gardening can also increase yield and variety.

Additionally, hoop houses and tunnel greenhouses can serve as a testbed for sustainable gardening practices. They are ideal for experimenting with water conservation techniques, integrated pest management, and even permaculture principles. By starting small and scaling up, gardeners can refine their skills and expand their horticultural knowledge.

In conclusion, tunnel greenhouses and hoop houses are versatile, cost-effective solutions for extending the growing season and enhancing plant protection. They offer a practical entry point into the world of greenhouse gardening, with plenty of scopes to grow and adapt these structures to meet a wide array of gardening needs and ambitions. Whether you're a hobbyist looking to extend your gardening season or a commercial grower aiming to maximize production, these greenhouses provide a robust framework for success in a variety of climatic conditions.

3.3. GLASS VS. POLYCARBONATE GREENHOUSES

When setting up a greenhouse, choosing between glass and polycarbonate materials is a critical decision that impacts not just the aesthetics of your garden but also its functionality and maintenance. Both materials have their unique strengths and potential drawbacks.

Glass Greenhouses: Classic Elegance with Clarity Glass has been the traditional choice for greenhouses for centuries, prized for its clarity and durability. It offers several distinct advantages:

- **Optimal Light Transmission**: Glass provides excellent clarity, allowing maximum sunlight to enter, which is crucial for plant growth.

- **Longevity**: Properly maintained glass can last for decades without losing transparency or strength.

- **Aesthetics**: Glass has a timeless appeal, offering a clear view of your plants and blending seamlessly into any garden setting.

However, glass also has some considerations that might be drawbacks for some gardeners:

- **Cost**: Glass greenhouses are generally more expensive to construct due to the material costs and the need for a strong frame to support the heavy glass.

- **Fragility**: Glass is prone to breaking when impacted, which can be a concern in areas with frequent severe weather or where accidental impacts are likely.

- **Energy Efficiency**: While glass excels in letting light in, it does not insulate as well as polycarbonate, which can lead to higher heating costs in colder climates.

Polycarbonate Greenhouses: Durable and Energy Efficient
Polycarbonate is a newer material in the realm of greenhouse gardening but has quickly gained popularity due to its unique properties:

- **Durability**: Unlike glass, polycarbonate is impact-resistant and less likely to break or shatter, making it ideal for areas prone to severe weather.

- **Insulation**: Polycarbonate typically comes in twin-wall sheets that trap air between layers, providing better insulation than single-pane glass. This can help maintain more stable temperatures within the greenhouse.

- **Light Diffusion**: The structure of polycarbonate diffuses light, which can help reduce the incidence of plant sunburn and ensure more even light distribution.

Polycarbonate does have some drawbacks:

- **Light Transmission**: While it diffuses light well, polycarbonate does not offer the same clarity as glass, which might affect the growth of plants that require direct sunlight.

- **Aging**: Over time, polycarbonate can yellow and become brittle if exposed to continual UV radiation without proper UV stabilization.

- **Aesthetic**: Some gardeners may find the look of polycarbonate less appealing than glass, as it can have a more utilitarian appearance.

Choosing the Right Material for Your Greenhouse Your choice between glass and polycarbonate should be informed by several factors:

- **Climate**: Consider the typical weather patterns in your area. Polycarbonate might be the better option in regions with harsh weather due to its durability and insulative properties, while glass could be ideal for milder climates.

- **Budget**: If cost is a significant concern, polycarbonate is usually less expensive and easier to install, which might sway your decision if you are working within a tight budget.

- **Aesthetics**: Think about how the greenhouse will complement your existing garden and home. Glass might be preferable if the visual appeal and traditional look are important to you.

- **Plant Types**: Consider what types of plants you intend to grow. Plants that require a lot of direct sunlight might benefit more from the clarity of glass, whereas polycarbonate might suffice for less fussy vegetation.

Ultimately, the choice between glass and polycarbonate for your greenhouse depends on a balance of aesthetic preferences, budget considerations, climate conditions, and your specific gardening needs. Both materials offer unique benefits that can help you create a thriving garden sanctuary.

CHAPTER 4: BUILDING OR BUYING YOUR GREENHOUSE

4.1. DIY GREENHOUSE BUILDING BASICS

Building your own greenhouse is an exciting project that merges gardening passion with a bit of construction fun. It's a rewarding endeavor that not only enhances your gardening capabilities but also personalizes your growing environment. Here's a guide to help you understand the basics of DIY greenhouse construction, ensuring you build a functional and enduring space for your plants.

Understanding the Basics

A DIY greenhouse provides a controlled environment where plants can thrive. Here are the key components and considerations to plan your build:

1. **Material Choice**: Decide between glass and polycarbonate for the covering. Glass offers longevity and clarity, while polycarbonate is shatter-resistant and provides good insulation with its twin-wall panels.

2. **Structural Frame**: Your greenhouse's frame can be made from wood, aluminum, or galvanized steel. Wood offers a classic look but requires maintenance to prevent decay. Aluminum and steel provide durability and require less upkeep.

3. **Foundation**: A solid foundation is crucial. Options range from simple wooden frames for small greenhouses to more elaborate concrete foundations for larger structures. Consider your climate; in colder regions, a deeper foundation may be necessary to prevent frost heave.

4. **Orientation**: Maximize sun exposure by positioning the greenhouse with a longer side facing south. This ensures ample sunlight during the day, crucial for plant growth.

5. **Insulation**: Proper insulation is vital for maintaining temperature. Use materials like polystyrene or bubble wrap on less sun-exposed sides to enhance thermal retention.

Step-by-Step Construction Guide

Planning and Preparation

- **Design Your Layout**: Sketch out your greenhouse dimensions and layout. Consider space for walking, storage, and plant growth.

- **Select a Location**: Choose a level site with good sun exposure and protection from strong winds. Ensure easy access to water and electricity if needed.

Building the Foundation

- **Clear and Level the Area**: Remove any debris, weeds, or turf. Level the ground to ensure a stable base.

- **Lay the Foundation**: Depending on your choice, lay a gravel bed, pour a concrete slab, or set up a wooden frame. Ensure it's perfectly level.

Constructing the Frame

- **Assemble the Frame**: Using your chosen material, construct the frame according to your design. Ensure all joints are securely fastened and stable.

- **Install Doors and Vents**: Fit doors and adjustable vents for adequate ventilation. Ensure they are well-sealed when closed.

Covering Installation

- **Install the Covering**: Attach your chosen material (glass or polycarbonate) to the frame. If using polycarbonate, ensure the channels are correctly oriented to prevent moisture buildup.

- **Seal and Secure**: Use appropriate sealants to prevent air leaks. Secure the panels with clips or screws designed for your covering material.

Finishing Touches

- **Internal Setup**: Install any internal structures such as shelves or planting beds.

- **Irrigation and Heating**: Set up an irrigation system for easy watering. Install heating if needed, especially in colder climates.

Maintenance and Upkeep

- **Regular Checks**: Inspect the structure regularly for damage or wear. Check for cracks, leaks, or loose panels and repair as necessary.

- **Cleaning**: Keep the glass or polycarbonate clean to maximize light penetration. Remove any algae or mold buildup promptly.

Tools and Materials Checklist

- Measuring tape, level, and square

- Drill, screws, and hammer

- Saw for cutting wood or metal (depending on frame material)

- Heavy-duty scissors or a utility knife for cutting polycarbonate

- Sealants and caulking gun

- Protective gloves and safety goggles

Building your own greenhouse is not just about providing a space for plants to grow; it's about creating a sanctuary where you can engage with nature regardless of the outside weather. With careful planning and execution, your DIY greenhouse can become a cornerstone of your gardening practice, providing a perfect environment for your plants to flourish.

4.2. CHOOSING AND ASSEMBLING A GREENHOUSE KIT

Selecting and assembling a greenhouse kit is an essential step towards realizing your gardening dreams. It's a process that combines practical decision-making with the excitement of starting a new gardening project. Here's a guide to help you choose the right greenhouse kit and assemble it effectively.

Choosing the Right Greenhouse Kit

1. Determine the Right Size

- **Space and Capacity**: Consider how much space you have in your garden and how much interior space you need for plants. Think about both your current and future gardening needs.

- **Scalability**: Some greenhouse kits can be expanded later with additional modules. This can be a cost-effective way to start small and grow your greenhouse as your needs increase.

2. Select the Appropriate Materials

- **Frame Materials**: Frames are typically made from aluminum, steel, or wood. Aluminum is lightweight and resistant to rust; steel is very sturdy and ideal for larger greenhouses; wood offers a classic look but requires maintenance to prevent decay.

- **Glazing Options**: Choose between glass, polycarbonate, or other plastics. Glass is durable and offers clear viewing but can be expensive and fragile. Polycarbonate is tough, provides good insulation, and is safer but can yellow over time.

3. Consider the Location

- **Sun Exposure**: Most plants need good sunlight. Place your greenhouse where it will receive maximum sunlight throughout the day. Avoid shady areas under trees or buildings.

- **Protection from Elements**: Ensure the location offers some natural protection from harsh winds and is not prone to pooling water.

4. Features to Look For

- **Ventilation**: Adequate ventilation is crucial for temperature control and preventing diseases. Look for kits with adjustable roof vents and side vents.

- **Access**: Ensure the greenhouse has easy access, preferably with a door that is wide enough to move plants and supplies in and out comfortably.

- **Shelving and Hanging Options**: Some greenhouses come with shelving or allow you to add shelves later. Think about the vertical space and how you can maximize it.

Assembling Your Greenhouse Kit

1. Prepare the Site

- **Clear the Area**: Remove any debris, weeds, or other obstructions from the site.

- **Level the Ground**: Ensure the ground is flat and level to avoid structural issues during and after assembly.

2. Lay the Foundation

- **Permanent Foundation**: For a more durable and stable structure, consider a concrete foundation. This is especially recommended for larger greenhouses.

- **Temporary Foundation**: For smaller or portable greenhouses, anchoring the frame to the ground with stakes or a wooden base may be sufficient.

3. Assemble the Frame

- **Follow Instructions**: Carefully read and follow the manufacturer's instructions. Each kit is different, and assembly steps can vary significantly.

- **Use Proper Tools**: Have all the necessary tools on hand before starting. Common tools needed include a screwdriver, hammer, wrench, and sometimes a drill.

4. Install the Glazing

- **Securely Attach Panels**: Start from one end and work your way to the other. Make sure each panel is securely fastened to the frame to withstand wind and weather.

- **Seal Gaps**: Use sealants where necessary to prevent air leaks, which can affect temperature control inside the greenhouse.

5. Add Finishing Touches

- **Install Internal Structures**: Add any internal shelves, hanging rods, or planting beds.

- **Check for Stability**: Ensure the greenhouse is stable and securely anchored to the foundation.

- **Final Inspection**: Walk around and inspect the greenhouse to make sure everything is in place, secure, and operational.

Starting Your Garden

Once your greenhouse is assembled, you can start planning the layout of your plants. Consider the needs of different plants regarding light and space, and arrange them accordingly. With your greenhouse now ready, you can look forward to a productive and enjoyable gardening experience, no matter the weather outside.

Assembling a greenhouse kit is a project that rewards careful planning and attention to detail with a versatile and functional space for gardening year-round. Enjoy the process, and happy gardening!

Buying a used greenhouse can be a fantastic way to save money and practice sustainability, but it requires careful consideration to ensure you get a structure that serves your gardening needs well. Here are some practical tips for evaluating and purchasing a used greenhouse:

1. Inspect the Frame

- **Material Condition**: Check the condition of the frame material, whether it's made of wood, aluminum, or steel. Look for signs of corrosion or rot, especially in joints and at ground contact points.

- **Structural Integrity**: Ensure the frame is structurally sound and free of major defects that could affect its stability or usability.

2. Evaluate the Glazing

- **Type of Material**: Identify whether the glazing is glass, polycarbonate, or another material. Each has different durability, light transmission, and insulation properties.

- **Condition**: Look for cracks, cloudiness, or any discoloration in the glazing. Check how securely the panels are fitted into the frame.

3. Check for Complete Components

- **Missing Parts**: Verify that all necessary components are present. Missing parts can be challenging to replace, especially for discontinued models.

- **Functionality**: Ensure that doors, vents, and windows open and close properly and that all hardware is operational.

4. Assess the Size

- **Space Requirements**: Make sure the greenhouse's size fits your available space and meets your gardening needs. Consider both the footprint and height of the structure.

5. Consider the Foundation

- **Existing Foundation**: If the greenhouse comes with a foundation, check its condition. Look for cracks or uneven settling, which might indicate issues.

- **Relocation Feasibility**: If you need to move the greenhouse, think about whether the foundation can be moved or if you'll need to construct a new one.

6. Evaluate the Location and Transportation

- **Current Location**: Inspect the site to understand how the greenhouse was situated in relation to sunlight, wind, and other environmental factors.

- **Transportation Cost**: Consider the cost and logistics of moving the greenhouse to your property. This can significantly affect the overall affordability.

7. Determine Upgrade and Repair Costs

- **Immediate Repairs**: Calculate the cost of any immediate repairs needed, such as replacing panels or structural elements.

- **Upgrades**: Consider whether you will need to invest in upgrades like automatic vent openers or new shading materials.

8. Inspect for Pests and Diseases

- **Signs of Infestation**: Look for signs of pest infestations or disease in the structure, which could transfer to your plants.

- **Treatment History**: Ask the seller about any past issues with pests or diseases and how they were treated.

9. Review Compliance with Local Regulations

- **Building Codes**: Check if the greenhouse meets local building codes and zoning regulations, which could affect your ability to use or modify the structure.

- **Permits**: Find out if you'll need permits to relocate and use the greenhouse on your property.

10. Negotiate Based on Total Cost

- **Consider All Expenses**: Factor in the cost of repairs, transportation, and any upgrades into your negotiation. Ensure the total cost is within your budget and reflects the greenhouse's condition and value.

Buying Considerations

Purchasing a used greenhouse offers the potential for great rewards but also comes with risks. By thoroughly inspecting the structure, evaluating its suitability for your needs, and calculating all associated costs, you can make an informed decision. Always approach the purchase with a clear understanding of what it will take to make the greenhouse functional for your specific gardening goals.

A used greenhouse not only allows you to extend your growing season but also aligns with eco-friendly practices by reusing materials and reducing waste. With careful consideration and planning, it can be a fulfilling addition to your gardening journey.

CHAPTER 5: GREENHOUSE ENVIRONMENT CONTROL

5.1. HEATING YOUR GREENHOUSE

Heating your greenhouse effectively is crucial for nurturing your plants through the colder months. Maintaining a consistent, warm environment not only extends your growing season but also protects your plants from potentially fatal temperature drops. Here's how to approach heating your greenhouse:

Understanding the Basics

Why Heat Your Greenhouse?

- **Plant Protection:** Many plants, especially tender or tropical ones, can suffer or die in cold temperatures. Heating provides a stable environment where they can thrive year-round.

- **Extended Growing Season:** Heat allows you to start seedlings earlier and grow plants for longer, potentially increasing your yields and gardening satisfaction.

Factors Affecting Greenhouse Heating

1. **Insulation:** Proper insulation is key to retaining heat efficiently. This includes having well-sealed doors, windows, and any other openings.

2. **Ventilation:** While keeping the greenhouse warm is important, proper ventilation is crucial to prevent overheating and to control humidity.

3. **Sun Exposure:** Maximizing sunlight can naturally help heat your greenhouse, reducing the reliance on artificial heating during daylight hours.

4. **External Climate:** The colder your local climate, the more heating power you will need to maintain optimal temperatures inside the greenhouse.

5. **Greenhouse Size and Volume:** Larger greenhouses will generally require more heat than smaller ones, as there is more space to keep warm.

Choosing the Right Heating System

1. Electric Heaters:

- **Pros:** Easy to install, provide clean and consistent heat.
- **Cons:** Can be expensive to operate, especially in areas with high electricity costs.

2. Gas Heaters (Natural Gas or Propane):

- **Pros:** Typically more cost-effective than electric heaters, can heat larger spaces efficiently.
- **Cons:** Require proper ventilation to prevent carbon monoxide buildup; installation can be more complex.

3. Paraffin Heaters:

- **Pros:** Inexpensive to run, good for smaller greenhouses.
- **Cons:** Produce combustion products that need to be vented; can leave soot and moisture that may harm some plants.

4. Biomass Heaters (Wood, Pellets):

- **Pros:** Can be economical, especially if you have access to cheap or free biomass.
- **Cons:** Requires manual feeding and regular maintenance; not suitable for unattended heating.

Tips for Efficient Greenhouse Heating

1. Optimize Insulation:

- Use bubble wrap or specially designed greenhouse insulation on the inside of the glass. This traps air and creates an insulating layer.

- Seal gaps around doors and windows to prevent drafts.

2. Use Thermal Mass:

- Water barrels or concrete blocks can absorb heat during the day and release it slowly at night, helping to stabilize temperature fluctuations.

3. Automate Where Possible:

- Install thermostats to control heaters automatically, ensuring they run only when necessary.

- Consider using timers on electric heaters to reduce energy consumption during off-peak hours.

4. Regular Maintenance:

- Keep heating systems clean and in good repair to ensure they operate at maximum efficiency.

- Check and replace filters in gas heaters to ensure they are not obstructed.

Safety Considerations

- **Ventilation:** Always ensure there is adequate ventilation when using gas or biomass heaters to avoid toxic build-ups of gases like carbon monoxide.

- **Fire Safety:** Keep flammable materials away from heaters and ensure electrical systems are professionally installed and maintained.

Conclusion

Choosing and maintaining an appropriate heating system for your greenhouse is vital for plant health and energy efficiency. By understanding the different types of heaters available and implementing strategies to enhance heat retention and efficiency, you can create a warm, thriving environment for your plants throughout the year. Remember to balance your heating needs with environmental and safety considerations to enjoy a productive and safe greenhouse gardening experience.

5.2. VENTILATION AND AIR CIRCULATION

Maintaining proper ventilation and air circulation in your greenhouse is crucial for creating a healthy environment where your plants can thrive. This not only helps regulate temperature and humidity but also ensures that your plants have access to the fresh air they need for photosynthesis.

Understanding the Importance of Ventilation

Ventilation in a greenhouse serves several vital functions:

- **Temperature Control**: It helps in maintaining an optimal temperature by allowing hot air to escape and cooler air to enter.

- **Humidity Regulation**: Proper airflow helps manage the humidity levels, reducing the risk of plant diseases associated with high moisture like mold and mildew.

- **CO2 and Oxygen Exchange**: Fresh air brings in carbon dioxide necessary for photosynthesis and helps to remove oxygen produced by plants.

Types of Greenhouse Ventilation

1. Natural Ventilation

- This involves using the structure of the greenhouse to facilitate air movement without mechanical aid. Features like roof vents, side vents, or roll-up sides can be used to create a flow of air driven by natural wind and thermal buoyancy.
- **Pros**: Energy-efficient, no operational costs.
- **Cons**: Less control over air movement, effectiveness dependent on weather conditions.

2. Forced Ventilation

- Utilizes fans and exhaust systems to control the airflow actively.
- **Pros**: Provides consistent airflow regardless of external conditions, can be controlled with thermostats and timers.
- **Cons**: Increased energy costs, requires maintenance of mechanical systems.

Optimizing Air Circulation

1. Strategic Placement of Vents and Fans

- Place vents or fans at opposite ends of the greenhouse to create a steady stream of air. Ensure that there are enough vents to cover about 15-20% of the floor area for effective cross-ventilation.
- Consider using circulation fans within the greenhouse to move air around plants, preventing the formation of air hotspots and promoting even growth.

2. Using Shade and Thermal Screens

- During hotter months, use shade cloths or thermal screens to prevent excessive heat buildup which can be vented effectively.

- These tools not only help in cooling but also reduce the workload on ventilation systems.

Adjusting Ventilation for Seasons

- **Spring and Summer**: Increase ventilation to manage higher temperatures and humidity. Automated vent openers can be invaluable during these months for regulating heat and ensuring continuous air exchange.

- **Fall and Winter**: Reduce ventilation to conserve heat but continue to ensure enough air exchange to prevent damp conditions. Insulate vents to prevent cold drafts.

Monitoring and Maintenance

- **Regular Checks**: Inspect and maintain ventilation equipment regularly to ensure it is functioning correctly. Clean vents and fans to prevent blockages that can reduce efficiency.

- **Monitoring Tools**: Use hygrometers and thermometers to keep a close watch on humidity and temperature levels within your greenhouse. Adjust your ventilation settings based on these readings to create the ideal environment for your plants.

Eco-Friendly Practices

- **Solar-Powered Fans**: Consider solar-powered ventilation systems to reduce energy usage and embrace sustainable practices.

- **Heat Recovery Ventilators (HRV)**: These systems can help reclaim heat from exhaust air in colder months, reducing heating requirements and energy consumption.

Conclusion

Effective ventilation and air circulation are not just about keeping the air moving; it's about creating a dynamic environment that responds to the needs of your plants and the challenges posed by external weather conditions. By strategically managing airflow and temperature, you can ensure that your greenhouse is a productive, healthy place for your plants all year round.

Managing humidity and condensation is crucial in a greenhouse environment, where excessive moisture can lead to plant diseases and poor growth conditions. Let's explore effective strategies to ensure optimal humidity levels and prevent unwanted condensation.

Understanding Humidity and Its Impacts

Humidity is the amount of water vapor present in the air. In a greenhouse, maintaining the right humidity level is essential for:

- **Plant Health**: Certain plants require specific humidity levels to thrive.

- **Disease Prevention**: High humidity can promote the growth of mold, mildew, and fungi.

- **Temperature Control**: Humidity affects the greenhouse temperature; moist air can make it feel warmer.

Tools for Managing Humidity

1. **Hygrometers and Humidity Controllers**: These devices measure and help control the humidity levels inside your greenhouse. They can be set to trigger ventilation or dehumidification systems automatically.

2. **Ventilation**: Proper ventilation is key to controlling humidity. Manual or automated vent systems can help release excess moisture.

3. **Dehumidifiers**: In regions with naturally high humidity or during seasons when external humidity is high, using a dehumidifier can help maintain optimal conditions inside the greenhouse.

Strategies to Prevent Condensation

Condensation occurs when warm, moist air meets cooler surfaces, turning water vapor into droplets. This can be problematic, as it can lead to water damage and create an environment conducive to disease.

1. **Improving Air Circulation**: Use fans to keep air moving and prevent it from settling on cooler surfaces. This helps reduce the chances of condensation by maintaining a more uniform temperature and humidity throughout the greenhouse.

2. **Heating**: Maintaining a slightly warmer temperature inside the greenhouse can prevent the interior surfaces from becoming cool enough to cause condensation. This is particularly effective during colder months.

3. **Insulation**: Insulating the walls, roof, and even the floor of your greenhouse can help maintain temperature consistency and reduce condensation.

4. **Watering Practices**: Water plants in the morning so that moisture has a chance to evaporate throughout the day rather than build up overnight.

Adjusting to Seasonal Changes

Humidity management is not a set-it-and-forget-it task. It requires adjustments based on seasonal variations:

- **Spring and Fall**: These transitional seasons often have fluctuating temperatures that can lead to varying humidity levels inside the greenhouse. Regular monitoring and adjustments to ventilation and heating are necessary.

- **Summer**: High temperatures can lead to increased evaporation and higher internal humidity. Enhanced ventilation and the use of shade cloths can help manage the internal climate.

- **Winter**: Cold air holds less moisture, which can reduce humidity levels. However, heating can quickly increase humidity, requiring careful balance through ventilation.

Regular Maintenance for Optimal Performance

To ensure your humidity control systems remain effective, regular maintenance is crucial:

- **Check and Clean Vents**: Ensure vents are clear of debris to maintain airflow efficiency.

- **Inspect Fans and Dehumidifiers**: Clean fans regularly and check dehumidifiers for proper function and capacity.

- **Monitor Seals and Insulation**: Look for any gaps or deterioration in seals and insulation that might affect temperature and humidity control.

Conclusion

Effective humidity and condensation management in your greenhouse involves a combination of proper equipment, regular maintenance, and seasonal adjustments. By understanding the unique needs of your plants and the dynamics of your greenhouse environment, you can create a thriving sanctuary that supports robust plant growth and minimizes the risk of disease. This not only contributes to a healthier plant life but also enhances your enjoyment and success in greenhouse gardening.

CHAPTER 6: LIGHTING AND IRRIGATION

6.1. UNDERSTANDING LIGHT REQUIREMENTS

Light is a fundamental element for plant growth, especially in greenhouse gardening, where controlling light becomes a crucial aspect of cultivating healthy plants. This section explores the critical aspects of light requirements and how they influence plant development.

The Importance of Light in Photosynthesis

Light serves as the primary energy source for photosynthesis, the process by which plants convert light into chemical energy. It affects various plant functions, including growth rate, flowering, and fruit production. Understanding and managing light in your greenhouse can significantly impact the health and productivity of your plants.

Types of Light Required by Plants

- **Quality of Light**: This refers to the color or wavelength of light. Plants primarily use blue and red wavelengths. Blue light promotes leafy growth, while red light is crucial for flowering and fruiting.

- **Quantity of Light**: This is the intensity or amount of light a plant receives. It determines how much energy plants can produce via photosynthesis. Both too little and too much light can hinder plant growth.

- **Duration of Light**: Also known as photoperiod, this is the amount of time a plant is exposed to light. The length of light exposure can trigger flowering in some plants and is species-dependent.

Measuring Light in Greenhouses

Using tools like a light meter can help you measure the intensity of light within your greenhouse. These devices are crucial for ensuring your plants receive the optimal amount of light for their specific needs.

Natural Light vs. Supplemental Lighting

While greenhouses are designed to maximize the capture of natural sunlight, there are times, especially during shorter winter days, when supplemental lighting may be necessary to meet the plants' light requirements.

1. **Natural Light**: The orientation and design of your greenhouse affect how much natural light your plants receive. A south-facing orientation usually maximizes light exposure in the northern hemisphere.

2. **Supplemental Lighting**: Options include LED lights, high-intensity discharge lamps, and fluorescents, each providing different intensities and spectra of light suitable for various growth stages and plant types.

Strategies for Optimizing Light Efficiency

- **Reflective Materials**: Installing reflective materials on walls or using reflective mulches can increase light availability to plants by bouncing light back onto them.

- **Adjustable Shades**: These can help manage light intensity, especially during the summer months when too much light can lead to heat buildup and burn plants.

- **Proper Plant Spacing**: Ensuring there is adequate space between plants will help maximize light penetration and reduce the risk of disease caused by poor air circulation.

Light Management for Different Plants

Different plants require different light conditions:

- **High Light Plants**: Such as tomatoes and peppers, need about 6-8 hours of direct sunlight daily.

- **Medium Light Plants**: Such as herbs and some flowers, require slightly less intensity or duration of light.

- **Low Light Plants**: Such as leafy greens and some ornamentals, can thrive with less intense light conditions.

Seasonal Considerations

The angle of sunlight changes with the seasons, affecting how much natural light enters your greenhouse. In the winter, when the sun is lower in the sky, light penetrates less directly. This might necessitate the use of supplemental lighting to ensure plants receive enough light.

Conclusion

Understanding and managing light requirements in a greenhouse setting is vital for successful plant growth. By measuring and adjusting light conditions, using the right type of supplemental lighting when necessary, and considering the specific needs of different plants, you can create an optimal growing environment that enhances plant health and productivity. This proactive approach to light management will ensure that your greenhouse gardening efforts are fruitful and rewarding.

6.2. SETTING UP GREENHOUSE LIGHTING SYSTEMS

Greenhouse lighting is crucial for supplementing natural sunlight, especially during shorter days or in cloudy climates. Proper lighting ensures that your plants receive the optimal light spectrum and intensity needed for growth. Here's a guide to setting up an effective lighting system in your greenhouse.

Understanding Light Needs

Before diving into lighting setups, assess the specific light requirements of your plants. Different species have varying needs regarding light intensity and spectrum. For example:

- **High Light Plants**: Such as tomatoes and peppers need more intense light.

- **Low Light Plants**: Such as ferns and some herbs can thrive with less.

Types of Greenhouse Lighting

1. **Fluorescent Lights**:

   - **Best for**: Seedlings and low-light plants.

   - **Benefits**: Energy efficient and emit low levels of heat.

   - **Setup Tips**: Hang them 6-12 inches above plants.

2. **LED Lights**:

   - **Best for**: Full-spectrum needs and all growth stages.

   - **Benefits**: Highly energy-efficient and have a long lifespan. They can be programmed to emit specific light wavelengths.

   - **Setup Tips**: Placement can vary; adjustable systems are ideal to cater to different plant heights and growth stages.

3. **High-Intensity Discharge (HID) Lights**:

   - **Types**: Metal Halide (MH) for vegetative growth and High-Pressure Sodium (HPS) for flowering.

   - **Benefits**: Covers larger areas due to high light output.

   - **Setup Tips**: They generate more heat and should be placed further from the plants, approximately 24-36 inches above.

Planning Your Lighting Layout

- **Uniform Coverage**: Ensure that lights are spaced to provide uniform coverage across all plants. Avoid hotspots and shaded areas as much as possible.

- **Adjustable Systems**: Consider systems that allow you to raise and lower lights easily, adapting to plant growth and seasonal changes.

- **Integration with Natural Light**: Optimize the use of natural light first, then supplement with artificial lighting based on the needs of your plants and local climate conditions.

Installation Tips

- **Electrical Safety**: Ensure all fixtures are suitable for humid environments and that wiring is professionally installed and safely routed.

- **Reflectors**: Use reflectors to maximize light efficiency, directing light downwards onto the plants rather than dispersing it sideways.

- **Timers**: Automate lighting with timers to provide consistent daily light intervals that mimic natural daylight hours, supporting your plants' natural growth cycles.

Monitoring and Maintenance

- **Regular Checks**: Regularly check and clean light fixtures to maintain high light output. Dust and dirt can significantly reduce efficiency.

- **Light Meters**: Use light meters to ensure your plants are receiving the proper light intensity and adjust your setup accordingly.

- **Observe Plant Responses**: Monitor how your plants respond to the lighting. Signs of too much light include leaf burn or bleaching, while insufficient light may result in elongated, weak stems and poor growth.

Energy Efficiency and Cost Management

- **Energy-Efficient Bulbs**: Opt for LEDs or energy-efficient fluorescents to reduce energy costs.

- **Solar Power Options**: Consider using solar panels to power lighting systems, reducing dependency on grid electricity and enhancing sustainability.

- **Cost-Effective Operations**: Balance the light requirements with energy costs by using lights only during necessary periods and leveraging natural light to the fullest.

By understanding the specific needs of your plants and using the right type of lighting, you can optimize growth and ensure your greenhouse thrives throughout the year. The key is to simulate natural environmental conditions as closely as possible, ensuring that your plants develop naturally and healthily.

6.3. EFFICIENT WATERING AND IRRIGATION SOLUTIONS

In greenhouse gardening, mastering artificial lighting is essential to ensure your plants receive enough light, especially during shorter daylight hours or in less sunny locales. Let's explore how to effectively set up lighting systems in your greenhouse to optimize plant growth and extend the growing season.

Essential Factors to Consider

1. Determine Light Requirements:

- **Plant Needs**: Different plants require varying light intensities. Understand the specific light needs of your plants—whether they are high-light plants like tomatoes or low-light plants like some herbs.

- **Sunlight Assessment**: Measure how much natural sunlight your greenhouse receives and determine if additional lighting is necessary.

2. Choose the Right Type of Lighting:

- **LEDs (Light Emitting Diodes)**: Highly efficient and long-lasting, LEDs can provide full-spectrum lighting, which is ideal for all growth stages. They generate less heat and can be placed closer to plants without the risk of heat damage.

- **Fluorescent Lighting**: Good for seedlings and low-light plants, these are energy-efficient but typically offer less intensity compared to LEDs.

- **HID (High-Intensity Discharge) Lights**: Including Metal Halide (MH) and High-Pressure Sodium (HPS) lamps, HIDs are powerful and effective for larger greenhouses but generate significant heat and consume more energy.

Lighting Setup Strategies

1. Configuration: Arrange lights to ensure even coverage across all plants. Avoid shadowing and ensure each plant receives adequate light.

2. Height and Positioning: Adjust the height of lights based on plant growth stages. Young seedlings might need lights placed closer compared to full-grown plants.

3. Timing: Use timers to replicate natural light cycles. Adjust light exposure according to the plant species and their growth stage needs.

Efficient Use of Lighting

1. Reflectors: Utilize reflectors to maximize light efficiency by directing light downwards towards the plants, reducing waste.

2. Energy Management: Consider energy-efficient lighting options like LEDs to reduce electricity usage. Monitor and optimize the operating times to balance energy consumption with plant health.

3. Heat Management: In setups where heat output from lights is significant (such as HID lights), ensure adequate ventilation to manage temperature and protect plants from heat stress.

Advanced Techniques

1. Light Metering: Use a light meter to measure the actual light levels at plant canopy level. Adjust your lighting setup based on these readings to ensure optimal light intensity.

2. Automated Systems: Implement smart lighting systems that can automatically adjust brightness and duration based on the time of day or the ambient light level outside the greenhouse.

Integration with Greenhouse Operations

Combine your lighting strategy with other greenhouse systems:

- **Ventilation**: Ensure proper airflow to manage heat from lights.

- **Irrigation**: Align watering schedules with light cycles. Plants may require more water as light intensity and duration increase.

- **Temperature Control**: Monitor temperature fluctuations caused by lighting systems and adjust heating or cooling as needed.

Setting up an efficient and effective lighting system in your greenhouse involves understanding the specific needs of your plants, choosing the right type of lighting, and strategically placing and managing these lights to maximize growth. By integrating smart technologies and efficient practices, you can significantly enhance the productivity of your greenhouse operations, ensuring that your plants thrive in an optimal growing environment.

7.1. CHOOSING THE RIGHT SOIL FOR YOUR GREENHOUSE

Selecting the ideal soil for your greenhouse is pivotal to ensuring your plants thrive. This crucial medium acts not just as a foundation, but as a dynamic contributor to the health and growth of your plants. Here's a comprehensive guide to understanding and choosing the right soil for your greenhouse gardening.

Understanding the Role of Soil in Greenhouses

Soil in a greenhouse does more than just hold plants in place. It is the primary medium that supplies nutrients, water, and oxygen to the plants. The right soil ensures proper root development, supports microbial life that benefits plant health, and helps manage water drainage and retention.

Key Components of Good Greenhouse Soil

1. **Texture**: The texture of the soil affects drainage and nutrient availability. Loamy soil, which is a balanced mix of sand, silt, and clay, is ideal as it retains nutrients and moisture but still drains well.

2. **Drainage and Water Retention**: Good greenhouse soil should drain excess water efficiently to prevent root diseases but also retain enough moisture to sustain the plants between waterings.

3. **Nutrient Content**: Soil should be rich in organic matter which provides nutrients to the plants and also improves soil structure and moisture retention.

4. **pH Level**: Most plants prefer a slightly acidic to neutral pH (6.0 to 7.0). The soil pH can significantly affect plant growth as it influences how plants absorb nutrients.

Customizing Soil for Greenhouse Use

Base Soil Mix: You can create a balanced base mix suitable for most plants using one part garden soil, one part compost (for nutrients), and one part sand (for drainage). This mix can be adjusted based on specific plant needs.

Adjusting Texture: If your base mix is too dense or clayey, adding sand or perlite can improve drainage. Conversely, if it's too sandy, adding compost or peat moss can help retain moisture.

Enhancing Nutrient Content: Incorporate compost, well-rotted manure, or a balanced slow-release fertilizer to enrich the soil. Regularly top up these nutrients, especially after growing heavy-feeding plants.

Managing pH: Test your soil's pH and adjust accordingly using lime to increase pH or sulfur to decrease pH. This adjustment should be based on the specific needs of the plants you intend to grow.

Best Practices for Soil Management in Greenhouses

1. **Regular Testing**: Regularly test your soil for pH and nutrient content. This will help you understand when to adjust your soil amendments and understand your soil's health over time.

2. **Sterilization**: Consider sterilizing your soil to eliminate diseases, weed seeds, and pests that could harm your plants. This can be done through solarization or by using commercial soil sterilizers.

3. **Mulching**: Apply organic mulch to conserve moisture, regulate soil temperature, and reduce weed growth. Mulch also gradually breaks down, adding organic matter to the soil.

4. **Rotation and Rest**: Rotate crops to prevent soil-borne diseases and nutrient depletion. Allow soil to rest or grow cover crops that can enrich the soil when not growing cash crops.

5. **Hydroponics**: For those looking to bypass soil issues, hydroponic systems can be an effective alternative, providing nutrients directly to the roots in a water solution.

Tailoring Soil to Specific Plant Types

Different plants have specific soil needs:

- **Succulents and Cacti**: Require sharp drainage. Mix coarse sand or gravel into your base mix.

- **Acid-Loving Plants**: Such as blueberries, need a lower pH. Amend soil with peat moss and sulfur to achieve the desired acidity.

- **Orchids and Tropical Plants**: May require special mixes that mimic their natural growing environments, often incorporating bark and charcoal.

Choosing the right soil for your greenhouse involves understanding the balance of texture, nutrients, and pH that your particular plants need. By customizing your soil mix and practicing regular soil management, you can create a thriving environment that supports robust plant growth. Remember, every plant's success starts from the ground up, so investing time and effort into developing the perfect soil mix will pay dividends in the health and productivity of your greenhouse garden.

Exploring soilless gardening methods like hydroponics and aquaponics can revolutionize how you manage your greenhouse, offering efficient and environmentally friendly alternatives to traditional soil-based gardening.

Hydroponics: The Soilless Marvel

Overview: Hydroponics is the practice of growing plants in a water-based, nutrient-rich solution, bypassing traditional soil. This method allows for precise control over nutrients and water, leading to more efficient plant growth.

Benefits:

- **Water Efficiency**: Uses significantly less water than soil-based gardening as water in hydroponic systems is recirculated.

- **Space Savings**: Enables vertical stacking of hydroponic systems, maximizing greenhouse space.

- **Controlled Nutrition**: Nutrients are dissolved in the water, providing plants direct access to essential minerals, which can increase growth rates and yields.

- **Fewer Pests and Diseases**: With no soil, the risk of soil-borne pests and diseases is greatly reduced.

Systems:

- **Nutrient Film Technique (NFT)**: Circulates a thin stream of water and nutrients over the roots of plants, which are held in channels that allow roots to access the solution.

- **Deep Water Culture (DWC)**: Plants are suspended in a solution of nutrient-rich water where the roots are directly immersed.

- **Ebb and Flow**: Temporarily floods the grow area with nutrient solution and then drains it back into the reservoir.

- **Aeroponics**: Mists the roots of plants with a nutrient solution, minimizing water use and increasing oxygen exposure to roots.

Aquaponics: Integrating Aquaculture and Hydroponics

Overview: Aquaponics combines raising aquatic animals such as fish, snails, or prawns with hydroponics, in a symbiotic environment.

Benefits:

- **Natural Fertilizers**: The waste produced by aquatic animals provides an organic nutrient source for the plants.

- **Enhanced Sustainability**: Combines the best of both worlds, using the waste from the aquaculture to feed plants, which in turn purify the water for the fish.

- **Diversity of Produce**: Not only can you harvest plants, but you also have the option of harvesting fish.

Key Components:

- **Fish Tank**: Where the aquatic animals are kept.

- **Settling Basin**: Captures uneaten food and detached biofilms, and is often the site where nitrification takes place.

- **Biofilter**: A location where nitrification bacteria can grow and convert ammonia into nitrates, which are excellent plant nutrients.

- **Hydroponics Subsystem**: Where plants are grown by absorbing excess nutrients from the water.

- **Sump**: The lowest point in the system, where the water flows to and from which it is pumped back to the aquaculture system.

Considerations:

- **Balancing Act**: The system needs to maintain a balance between the number of fish and the capacity of the plants to utilize the nutrients they provide.

- **Water Quality**: Regular monitoring and adjustment to ensure the health of both fish and plants.

- **Learning Curve**: Requires understanding both aquaculture and hydroponic systems, which can be complex for beginners.

Setting Up Your System

Getting Started:

- **Research**: Thoroughly understand the needs of the plants and fish you want to cultivate.

- **System Design**: Choose a system that fits your space and meets the needs of your chosen plants and fish.

- **Monitoring and Adjustments**: Regularly check and adjust water pH, nutrient levels, and system flow to ensure optimal growth conditions.

Challenges:

- **Initial Costs**: Setup can be costly due to the need for pumps, grow beds, tanks, and proper plumbing systems.

- **Maintenance**: Requires regular feeding of fish, monitoring of water quality, and system maintenance.

Hydroponics and aquaponics represent innovative approaches to greenhouse gardening, minimizing dependency on soil and maximizing both space and resource efficiency. These systems not only challenge conventional gardening practices but also encourage a sustainable approach to food production, highlighting the harmony between technology and nature in modern agriculture.

7.3. CONTAINERS AND PLANTING BEDS

Choosing the right containers and planting beds is crucial for the success of your greenhouse gardening. This choice affects not just the health of your plants but also the efficiency and functionality of your gardening efforts. Let's explore how to select and utilize these essential components effectively.

Understanding Containers and Planting Beds

Containers and planting beds serve as the foundational environments for your plants. They determine root space, influence water drainage, affect soil temperature, and impact overall plant health.

Containers:

- **Materials**: Options include plastic, clay, fabric, and wood, each with specific benefits and drawbacks. Plastic is lightweight and retains moisture well but can degrade over time. Clay pots offer excellent breathability but are heavier and breakable. Fabric pots promote air pruning and superior drainage. Wooden containers are durable and have aesthetic appeal but can rot without proper treatment.

- **Size and Shape**: The size should match the root system of the plant; larger plants require deeper pots to accommodate their root growth. The shape can influence the plant's exposure to sunlight and water distribution.

Planting Beds:

- **Raised Beds**: These are ideal for managing soil quality and improving drainage. They also make it easier to control pests and weeds.

- **In-ground Beds**: These may be used where temperature control is not an issue, and the natural soil is of good quality. They are generally less costly to set up than raised beds.

- **Mobile Beds**: On casters or wheels, these beds can be moved to optimize light exposure throughout the seasons or to rearrange the greenhouse layout.

Selecting the Right Setup

Climate Considerations:

- In cooler climates, darker containers may help absorb and retain heat.

- In warmer regions, lighter colors or breathable materials like fabric can prevent roots from overheating.

Plant Specific Needs:

- Deep-rooted vegetables like tomatoes and carrots may require taller containers or deeper beds.

- Herbs and lettuce, which have shallower roots, can thrive in smaller or shallower containers.

Aesthetic Preferences:

- Consider the visual layout of your greenhouse. Coordinated or creatively mixed container styles can enhance the visual appeal of the space.

- Planting beds can be designed to create functional and beautiful patterns that make the greenhouse a pleasant space to work in.

Installation and Maintenance Tips

Drainage:

- Ensure all containers have adequate drainage to prevent waterlogging. Consider layering the bottom with gravel or permeable materials before adding soil.

- Raised beds should have a layer of landscape fabric or similar material to separate the soil from the base and facilitate proper drainage.

Soil Quality:

- Mix the appropriate type of soil for the plants you are growing. Containers often require a lighter, well-draining mix that might include components like perlite or coconut coir.

- Regularly amend the soil in both containers and beds with compost or other organic matter to maintain fertility.

Accessibility and Ergonomics:

- Ensure that all areas of your planting beds are easily reachable without needing to step into them, which can compact the soil.

- Consider elevated raised beds or taller containers to reduce the need to bend down, making gardening more comfortable and accessible.

Integrating into Greenhouse Management

Watering Systems:

- Automate watering with drip irrigation systems tailored for containers and beds to optimize water use and ensure consistent moisture levels.

- Monitor soil moisture using sensors to adjust watering schedules based on actual need rather than fixed timers.

Companion Planting:

- Utilize the concept of companion planting within larger containers or beds to maximize space and enhance plant health. For example, tomatoes grow well with basil, which can help repel harmful insects.

Seasonal Adjustments:

- Rotate crops in planting beds to prevent soil depletion and reduce pest buildup.

- Move containers around within the greenhouse to take advantage of changing light conditions throughout the year.

By carefully selecting and managing containers and planting beds, you can create a highly productive and efficient greenhouse environment. This foundation supports not just the physical growth of your plants but also contributes to a sustainable gardening practice that maximizes both yield and enjoyment.

CHAPTER 8: PLANT SELECTION AND CARE

8.1. HERBS, VEGETABLES, AND FRUITS FOR GREENHOUSE GROWING

Embarking on the journey of greenhouse gardening opens up a world of possibilities for cultivating a diverse array of herbs, vegetables, and fruits under a controlled environment. Here, we'll explore the best plants for greenhouse cultivation and offer guidance on how to ensure they thrive.

Herbs: Aromatic Essentials

Herbs are a delightful addition to any greenhouse, offering not just culinary benefits but also aromatic pleasure and ease of growth. Here's a closer look at some essential herbs suited for greenhouse cultivation, along with tips on how to maximize their growth and flavor.

1. Basil

Basil is a warm-weather herb that loves the stable environment of a greenhouse. With its preference for warm, sunny conditions, basil thrives when given ample sunlight or supplemental light. It requires regular watering but does not like to sit in water, so well-draining soil is crucial. For continuous growth, pinch off the flowering tops to encourage the plant to become bushier and produce more leaves. Common varieties include Sweet Basil, Thai Basil, and Purple Basil, each offering unique flavors for different culinary uses.

2. Chives

Chives are perennial herbs that are exceptionally easy to grow and maintain in a greenhouse setting. They prefer full sun but will tolerate partial shade, making them adaptable to various greenhouse locations. Chives can be harvested by cutting the leaves a few inches above the base of the plant. This herb adds a mild onion-like flavor to dishes and grows back quickly, making it a sustainable choice for regular harvesting.

3. Mint

Mint is known for its vigorous growth and can become invasive if not contained. In a greenhouse, growing mint in individual pots can help manage its spread while still enjoying its robust flavor. Mint prefers a slightly moist environment and partial shade to full sun. Frequent harvesting encourages it to grow fuller and more lush. Popular varieties include Spearmint and Peppermint, each with distinct tastes suitable for teas, desserts, and savory dishes.

4. Cilantro

Cilantro thrives in cooler greenhouse conditions and can be sown directly into the soil or started in containers. It enjoys a sunny spot but appreciates a bit of shade during the hottest part of the day. Cilantro tends to bolt quickly under warm conditions, so regular seeding every few weeks can ensure a continuous supply. Its leaves are perfect for fresh salsas, Asian, and Latin dishes, while the seeds (coriander) are used in spice mixes.

5. Parsley

Parsley is a biennial herb often grown as an annual in greenhouses. It prefers rich, well-draining soil and can be grown under full sun to partial shade. Parsley needs consistent moisture to thrive, so regular watering is essential. Both curly and flat-leaf varieties are popular, each bringing a fresh, clean flavor to dishes like soups, salads, and marinades.

6. Thyme

Thyme is a hardy, drought-resistant herb that thrives in well-draining soil and full sun. In a greenhouse, thyme can be grown in pots or directly in the ground. It benefits from minimal watering once established, making it a low-maintenance option for busy gardeners. Thyme's pungent flavor makes it a staple in Mediterranean cuisine, especially in dishes featuring lamb, poultry, and tomatoes.

Cultivation Tips

- **Soil Quality**: Use a high-quality, well-draining potting mix to prevent waterlogging, which can lead to root diseases.

- **Spacing**: Give each herb enough space to grow. This not only helps with air circulation but also reduces competition for nutrients.

- **Feeding**: Feed your herbs with a balanced, water-soluble fertilizer every few weeks to ensure they receive all the necessary nutrients for growth.

- **Pruning**: Regular pruning not only helps to keep the plants healthy and bushy but also encourages the production of new, flavorful leaves.

Vegetables: Versatile and Nutritious

Cultivating vegetables in a greenhouse is a rewarding endeavor that extends the growing season and increases yield through controlled environmental conditions. Here's a deeper exploration of the most versatile and nutritious vegetables for greenhouse growing, along with strategic tips to help them thrive.

1. Tomatoes

Tomatoes are a greenhouse staple due to their high yield and the superior taste of greenhouse-grown varieties. They prefer warm temperatures and consistent moisture. When growing tomatoes in a greenhouse, choose varieties that are bred for indoor environments, such as 'Cherry' for small, quick fruits or 'Beefsteak' for larger, meatier options. Staking or using trellises can help manage their vigorous growth and support the weight of the fruit.

2. Peppers

Both sweet and hot peppers excel in the stable warmth of a greenhouse. Peppers demand a long, warm growing season, which a greenhouse environment can consistently provide. They require staking for support as the fruits develop, and regular feeding with a high-potassium fertilizer once they begin to flower and fruit. Popular choices include bell peppers for their sweet, robust flavor and jalapeños or habaneros for those who prefer a spicy kick.

3. Leafy Greens

Leafy greens like lettuce, spinach, and kale are ideal for cooler parts of the greenhouse. These crops prefer shorter days and cooler temperatures, making them perfect for early spring and late autumn production. Leafy greens can be harvested leaf-by-leaf to extend the crop production or cut at the base for a full harvest. They benefit from frequent, light watering and minimal feeding.

4. Cucumbers

Cucumbers are well-suited to greenhouse cultivation, especially when trellised to encourage vertical growth, saving space and increasing air circulation around the plants. They thrive in warm, humid conditions but require consistent watering to prevent stress, which can lead to bitter fruits. Varieties like 'Slicer' for salads and 'Pickling' cucumbers for preserving are excellent choices.

5. Eggplants

Eggplants thrive in high temperatures, which makes them excellent candidates for summertime greenhouse growing. Like tomatoes, they need staking to support their tall stems and heavy fruits. Eggplants are relatively heavy feeders, requiring regular applications of a balanced fertilizer. Varieties such as 'Black Beauty' or 'Long Purple' provide bountiful and visually appealing fruits.

6. Carrots

Carrots can be grown in a greenhouse where soil conditions can be perfectly managed to avoid the stony soil that stunts growth in traditional gardens. They prefer loose, sandy soil that allows for deep root development. Carrots need little maintenance beyond regular watering, making them a good choice for gardeners of all skill levels.

7. Zucchini

Zucchini grows quickly and can produce a large yield from just a few plants, making it a space-efficient crop for greenhouse growing. It requires ample space for sprawling or can be trained up a support to conserve space. Consistent watering and feeding, particularly with a high-potassium fertilizer once flowering begins, will help ensure a robust harvest.

Advanced Tips for Growing Vegetables in a Greenhouse:

- **Pollination**: Many greenhouse vegetables, like tomatoes and cucumbers, benefit from manual pollination if natural pollinators are not present. This can be done using a small brush to transfer pollen from flower to flower.

- **Pest Management**: Keep an eye out for common greenhouse pests such as aphids, spider mites, and whiteflies. Use organic pest control methods such as introducing beneficial insects, using insecticidal soaps, or manual removal.

- **Climate Control**: Install fans or open vents to manage temperature and humidity, reducing the risk of disease and promoting healthy plant growth.

- **Soil Health**: Rotate crops annually to prevent soil-borne diseases and manage nutrient levels. This practice keeps the soil healthy and reduces the buildup of pathogens.

- **Water Management**: Use a drip irrigation system to deliver water directly to the base of each plant. This method is efficient and conserves water by reducing evaporation.

Fruits: Sweet and Luscious Treats for Greenhouse Cultivation

Expanding your greenhouse to include fruit cultivation can transform your gardening experience into a more diverse and rewarding endeavor. Fruits not only add a burst of sweetness and color to your greenhouse but also provide a delightful challenge for those looking to diversify their green thumb portfolio. Here's a detailed exploration of suitable fruits for greenhouse growing, along with expert tips for nurturing these sweet, luscious treats.

1. Strawberries

Strawberries are one of the most popular fruits for greenhouse growing due to their compact growth habit and the ability to produce fruit quickly. For year-round production, opt for everbearing varieties like 'Albion' or 'Day Neutral,' which don't rely on day length to flower. Hanging baskets or tiered planters maximize space and improve air circulation around the plants, reducing disease risk. Regular feeding with a balanced fertilizer and ensuring consistent moisture will help maximize yield.

2. Grapes

Growing grapes in a greenhouse can shield the vines from diseases and pests common in outdoor cultivation, allowing for cleaner, more bountiful harvests. Choose varieties like 'Lakemont' or 'Muscat of Alexandria,' which are well-suited to the confined space of a greenhouse. Grapes require a sturdy trellis system for support and benefit from strategic pruning to maximize sun exposure and air circulation around the clusters.

3. Figs

Figs thrive in warm conditions, making them ideal for greenhouse cultivation. Varieties like 'Brown Turkey' and 'Celeste' can produce fruit without pollination. Figs need large pots to accommodate their root systems and enjoy a heavy mulch layer to maintain soil moisture. Pruning is essential to keep the tree's size manageable and to encourage the growth of new fruit-bearing shoots.

4. Citrus

Citrus trees such as lemons, limes, and oranges can be successfully grown in greenhouses where temperatures are controlled. Dwarf varieties are best suited for pot culture, and their container mobility allows for easy adjustment within the greenhouse to maximize light exposure. Citrus trees require well-draining soil and benefit from regular feeds with citrus-specific or high-potassium fertilizers to support fruiting.

5. Peaches and Nectarines

Peaches and nectarines can be grown in a greenhouse environment, where they are protected from frost and peach leaf curl, a common disease. Dwarf varieties are preferable, and they need a deep, fertile soil to thrive. Pruning not only helps to maintain a manageable size but also encourages the growth of fruiting wood.

6. Melons

Melons, such as cantaloupes and honeydew, can excel in the warm, controlled environment of a greenhouse. They require a lot of space to sprawl; however, vertical trellising can save floor space and promote healthier plants. Melons benefit from consistent watering and regular applications of a high-potassium fertilizer as fruits develop.

Advanced Tips for Growing Fruits in a Greenhouse:

- **Pollination**: Fruits like strawberries and citrus are self-fertile, but others, especially melons, may require manual pollination if natural pollinators are absent in the greenhouse environment. Use a small paintbrush to transfer pollen from flower to flower.

- **Climate Control**: Maintain optimal temperatures and humidity levels to prevent stress and promote healthy growth. Excessive heat can be as detrimental as the cold for some fruiting plants.

- **Pest and Disease Management**: Regularly inspect plants for signs of pests or diseases. Organic methods, such as neem oil or introducing beneficial insects like ladybugs, can effectively manage pests without harming the plants.

- **Soil and Water Management**: Ensure that soil is well-draining to prevent root diseases and adjust watering schedules according to the plant's stage of growth—less water during dormancy and more during fruiting.

- **Pruning and Training**: Proper pruning not only manages plant size but also improves air circulation and light penetration, which are crucial for fruit development. Training vines and branches on trellises or against walls can also help maximize space and expose more of the plant to light.

- **Feeding**: Use a balanced fertilizer during the growth phase and switch to a high-potassium fertilizer closer to fruiting to enhance fruit quality and taste.

Incorporating fruit plants into your greenhouse not only enhances its biodiversity but also elevates the sensory pleasure of gardening, with the added bonus of fresh, sweet fruits right at your fingertips. Each fruit species offers unique benefits and requires specific care, but the overarching principles of good light, sufficient water, nutrient management, and pest control hold true. Embrace these practices, and you'll enjoy the lush, flavorful rewards of your greenhouse garden.

8.2. SEASONAL PLANTING AND CROP ROTATION

In the verdant world of greenhouse gardening, understanding and managing the cyclical nature of seasons is crucial for optimizing the health and yield of your crops. Seasonal planting and crop rotation not only align with these natural cycles but also enhance soil health, disrupt pest and disease cycles, and improve crop diversity. This approach ensures a sustainable and productive gardening experience.

Seasonal Planting in a Greenhouse

Unlike outdoor gardening, a greenhouse provides the unique ability to extend growing seasons and control environmental factors. This allows for more flexibility in planting schedules and the cultivation of a wider variety of plants throughout the year.

Winter:

- **Cool-weather crops** thrive in the winter greenhouse environment. Consider growing leafy greens like spinach, kale, and Swiss chard, which can tolerate lower temperatures.

- **Root vegetables** such as carrots and beets can also be successfully grown during the cooler months, benefiting from the greenhouse's protection from frost.

Spring:

- Spring is ideal for **starting seedlings** and transitioning to warmer-weather crops as the days lengthen and temperatures rise.

- Plant early-season vegetables such as peas, lettuce, and radishes, which can be harvested quickly before the hottest months.

Summer:

- Focus on heat-loving plants like tomatoes, cucumbers, and peppers. These plants benefit from the maximum light and controlled heat within the greenhouse.

- Utilize shading and ventilation to manage interior temperatures and protect plants from excessive heat.

Autumn:

- As temperatures begin to drop, transition to cool-season crops once again. This is a great time to start second plantings of greens or root vegetables.

- Prepare for overwintering plants or beginning crops like garlic and onions which will mature in the spring.

Crop Rotation

Rotating crops in a greenhouse is as essential as in outdoor gardening for maintaining soil health and preventing pest and disease build-up. Here's how to implement an effective crop rotation strategy:

1. **Divide the greenhouse into sections** based on the type of crops or the family to which they belong.

2. **Rotate crops from different families** to different sections each year. For example, follow tomatoes (a nightshade) with leafy greens (like lettuce) rather than another nightshade like peppers.

3. **Plan your rotation** based on crop needs and the nutrients they require. Legumes, for instance, can fix nitrogen and are beneficial to follow with nitrogen-hungry leafy greens.

Benefits of Seasonal Planting and Crop Rotation

- **Enhanced Soil Health:** Rotating crops helps prevent soil depletion by varying the plant demands placed on the soil. Different plants require and deposit different nutrients, thus balancing soil fertility.

- **Pest and Disease Management:** Crop rotation disrupts the life cycles of pests and diseases that thrive under continuous cropping conditions. By changing the crop environment, pests and diseases are less likely to establish and become problematic.

- **Increased Biodiversity:** Planting a variety of crops can increase biodiversity in your greenhouse, which can help attract beneficial insects and improve overall plant health.

- **Optimal Use of Space:** Seasonal planting maximizes the use of space throughout the year, allowing for continuous production. This is especially beneficial in limited spaces typical of greenhouse environments.

Implementing the Strategy

- **Keep detailed records** of what you plant and where each season to track crop rotation and planting schedules.

- **Adjust plans annually** based on observations and outcomes from the previous year. This will help refine your approach to meet the specific needs of your greenhouse environment.

- **Incorporate companion planting** to enhance crop rotation benefits. Certain plants can improve the growth of others by attracting beneficial insects, providing shade, or suppressing weeds.

By embracing the principles of seasonal planting and crop rotation, greenhouse gardeners can create a more resilient and productive garden. This strategic approach not only aligns with natural ecological processes but also enhances the gardening experience through improved crop health and yield.

In the realm of greenhouse gardening, understanding the cyclical nature of the seasons is akin to tapping into the natural rhythm of life itself. Seasonal planting and crop rotation in your greenhouse are quintessential practices that mirror these cycles, providing a sustainable and efficacious method to cultivate an array of produce throughout the year. This symbiotic relationship with nature not only nurtures the plants but also fortifies the soil, wards off pest invasions, and mitigates plant diseases, fostering a harmonious greenhouse environment.

Embracing the Seasons: A Greenhouse Gardener's Guide

Unlike traditional outdoor gardening, where planting schedules are tightly bound to the whims of the weather, greenhouses offer a unique advantage. They allow you to extend growing seasons and manipulate environmental conditions to benefit different types of plants throughout the year.

Winter

The cold months are perfect for growing cool-season crops that can tolerate or even prefer lower temperatures. Options include:

- **Leafy greens:** Spinach, kale, and Swiss chard can thrive in the cool environment of a winter greenhouse.

- **Root vegetables:** Carrots, radishes, and beets also do well, as they can handle the cooler soil temperatures.

Spring

As the outside temperature begins to warm, your greenhouse is ideal for starting seedlings and prepping for more temperature-sensitive plants:

- **Early starters:** Tomatoes, peppers, and cucumbers started in late winter can now begin to flourish.

- **Spring greens:** Lettuce and other salad greens can continue to grow before the heat of summer sets in.

Summer

This is the peak growing season when sunlight and warmth are abundant:

- **Heat lovers:** Plants that thrive in warmth, like tomatoes, cucumbers, and peppers, will produce well.

- **Continuous planting:** Keep starting fast-growing, heat-tolerant plants for continuous yields.

Autumn

As the heat wanes, shift back to crops that prefer cooler temperatures:

- **Late season crops:** Begin sowing fall-harvested vegetables like broccoli and cauliflower.

- **Preparation for winter:** Start planning for overwintering crops or begin growing winter greens.

Crop Rotation: Maximizing Health and Yield

Crop rotation is a crucial strategy in managing greenhouse cultivation, helping to maintain soil health and prevent disease and pest cycles:

- **Nutrient management:** Different plants have varying nutrient needs; rotating them helps prevent soil depletion.

- **Disease and pest deterrence:** Many pests and diseases are plant-specific. Rotating crops helps break these cycles, reducing the likelihood of infestation and infection.

Implementing Crop Rotation

1. **Plan your space:** Divide your greenhouse into sections based on the crop type.

2. **Rotate families:** Avoid planting the same family of crops in the same section consecutively. For example, after growing tomatoes (a nightshade), plant a legume to help fix nitrogen in the soil.

3. **Keep records:** Detailed notes on what you plant and where each season will help you manage rotation effectively and observe patterns in plant health and productivity.

Benefits of Seasonal Planting and Crop Rotation

- **Soil health:** Rotating crops helps improve soil structure and fertility by varying plant demands and reducing the buildup of pathogens.

- **Pest and disease control:** Crop rotation disrupts the life cycle of pests and diseases, reducing reliance on chemical interventions.

- **Yield optimization:** By aligning crop types with their optimal growing seasons within the controlled environment of a greenhouse, you can maximize both the health of your plants and your yields.

Seasonal planting and crop rotation are more than just traditional farming techniques adapted to the greenhouse; they are essential components of a sustainable gardening practice that respects the natural rhythms of the environment while optimizing for productivity and plant health. By thoughtfully planning and implementing these strategies, greenhouse gardeners can enjoy a diverse, healthy, and bountiful garden all year round.

CHAPTER 9: PEST AND DISEASE MANAGEMENT

9.1. IDENTIFYING COMMON GREENHOUSE PESTS

In the world of greenhouse gardening, understanding the vital role of pollination, along with diligent plant health management, is crucial for maintaining a vibrant and productive environment. Here's a comprehensive guide to mastering these aspects to enhance the health and yield of your greenhouse plants.

Understanding Pollination in a Greenhouse Environment

Pollination involves the transfer of pollen from the male parts of a flower to the female parts, leading to fertilization and the production of seeds. In the natural environment, this process is aided by wind, insects, and birds. However, in the enclosed space of a greenhouse, these natural pollinators are often absent, and manual intervention may become necessary.

For self-pollinating plants like tomatoes and peppers, a simple shake of the plant can suffice to distribute pollen. For others that require cross-pollination, such as cucumbers and squash, hand-pollination using a small brush or even your finger can effectively transfer pollen from flower to flower.

Promoting Healthy Pollination

To facilitate effective pollination in your greenhouse:

- **Attract Natural Pollinators:** Introducing plants that attract bees or butterflies can help bring natural pollinators into your space. Consider installing insect-friendly features like bee hotels to encourage their presence.

- **Use Pollination Assistants:** For larger or more professional setups, employing bumblebees can be a very effective way to ensure pollination. These pollinators are particularly effective in a greenhouse environment and can significantly increase the yield of crops like tomatoes.

Vigilant Plant Health Management

Keeping your plants healthy involves more than just regular watering and fertilizing. It encompasses comprehensive strategies to prevent disease, manage pests, and ensure optimal plant development.

Monitoring Plant Health

Regularly inspect your plants for signs of stress or disease. Look for symptoms like discoloration, spots on leaves, or stunted growth. Early detection is key to managing potential issues before they escalate.

Integrated Pest Management (IPM)

Implementing an IPM strategy involves using a combination of biological, cultural, mechanical, and chemical management tools to control pest populations effectively. This approach helps reduce the reliance on chemical pesticides, promoting a more sustainable environment.

Environmental Control

Maintaining the right temperature, humidity, and ventilation is crucial in preventing stress and disease in plants. Use fans, heaters, and humidifiers or dehumidifiers to create the ideal growing conditions for your specific plants.

Nutrient Management

Ensuring your plants receive the correct balance of nutrients can significantly affect their health and productivity. Use soil tests to guide your fertilization strategy, applying the right type and amount of nutrients at the appropriate stages of plant growth.

Dealing with Common Greenhouse Pests

Be on the lookout for pests that commonly infiltrate greenhouses, such as aphids, spider mites, whiteflies, and thrips. Here's how to manage them:

- **Preventive Measures:** Keep your greenhouse clean and free of plant debris where pests can breed. Use screens on air intakes to prevent pests from entering.

- **Biological Controls:** Introduce beneficial insects like ladybugs or lacewings, which prey on harmful pests.

- **Chemical Controls:** If necessary, use targeted pesticides as a last resort. Opt for organic or less harmful options to minimize impact on beneficial insects and the overall environment.

Regular Maintenance and Care

Consistent care and maintenance of your greenhouse and its inhabitants can prevent many problems associated with pests and plant diseases. This includes:

- **Cleaning Tools and Pots:** Regularly clean and sterilize gardening tools and pots to prevent the spread of disease.

- **Crop Rotation:** Rotate crops to prevent soil-borne diseases and reduce pest buildup.

- **Proper Watering Techniques:** Over-watering can lead to root rot and other moisture-related diseases. Ensure your watering methods provide adequate moisture without saturating the soil.

By understanding and implementing effective pollination techniques and plant health management strategies, you can ensure that your greenhouse remains a thriving, productive environment. This proactive approach not only enhances the health and yield of your plants but also makes your gardening practice more enjoyable and rewarding.

9.2. ORGANIC PEST CONTROL METHODS

In the tranquil environment of a greenhouse, the orchestration of an effective organic pest control strategy plays a pivotal role in maintaining plant health and ensuring a productive garden. This approach emphasizes a holistic relationship with nature, using methods that sustain the ecological balance and promote biodiversity.

Organic Pest Control Strategies

1. Introduce Beneficial Predators

- Introducing beneficial insects like ladybugs, lacewings, and predatory mites can naturally reduce the population of harmful pests like aphids, spider mites, and thrips. These natural predators can be a cornerstone of greenhouse pest management.

2. Companion Planting for Pest Control

- Utilize companion planting to deter pests naturally. Certain plants can repel unwanted insects or even improve the growth and flavor of other plants. For example, planting marigolds can deter nematodes, while basil can help repel thrips and mosquitoes.

3. Physical Barriers

- Employing physical barriers such as insect netting or floating row covers can effectively keep pests out without the need for chemical treatments. These barriers prevent pests from reaching the plants while still allowing light and air to pass through.

4. Homemade Organic Sprays

- Create organic sprays using common kitchen ingredients. A solution of water mixed with neem oil, garlic, or mild soap can act as an effective foliar spray to control small infestations of aphids, mites, and other pests.

5. Diatomaceous Earth

- Use diatomaceous earth as a non-toxic option to control pests. This fine powder creates a barrier that is lethal to insects with exoskeletons, such as ants, slugs, and beetles, by dehydrating them.

6. Biological Insecticides

- Consider biological insecticides like Bacillus thuringiensis (Bt) for controlling caterpillar pests, or Spinosad for broader insect control. These natural products disrupt the pests' lifecycle without harming beneficial insects or the environment.

Implementing Organic Pest Control

Regular Monitoring

- Consistent monitoring of your plants is crucial for early detection of pests. Inspect your plants regularly for signs of damage and presence of pests, and apply organic control methods promptly to prevent outbreaks.

Cultural Practices

- Maintain good cultural practices such as proper plant spacing, which ensures adequate air circulation and reduces the humidity that many pests thrive in. Removing plant debris and weeding regularly can also reduce pest habitats.

Soil Health

- Enhancing soil health can naturally suppress disease and reduce pest problems. Incorporate organic matter regularly, maintain soil pH, and use mulches to improve soil structure and encourage beneficial microbial activity.

Water Management

- Proper watering techniques can influence pest outbreaks, as overwatering can lead to root diseases and under-watering can stress plants, making them more susceptible to pests. Use watering methods that keep leaves dry, such as drip irrigation, to prevent the spread of disease.

Benefits of Organic Pest Control

- **Environmental Impact:** Reduces chemical runoff and residues in the environment.

- **Safety:** Safer for you, your family, and beneficial wildlife in and around your greenhouse.

- **Sustainability:** Promotes a sustainable approach to gardening that improves soil and plant health over time.

By embracing organic pest control methods, you not only protect your plants but also contribute to a healthier ecosystem within your greenhouse. These practices, while sometimes requiring more initial effort and observation, pay off by creating a robust garden that supports itself with minimal intervention.

9.3. PREVENTING AND MANAGING PLANT DISEASES

In the sanctuary of a greenhouse, where diverse plant life thrives under controlled conditions, the management of plant diseases plays a critical role in maintaining a healthy environment. This chapter will explore essential strategies for preventing and managing plant diseases, ensuring your greenhouse remains a bastion of growth and vitality.

Understanding Plant Diseases

Understanding the intricacies of plant diseases within the controlled environment of a greenhouse is crucial for maintaining the health and vitality of your plants. Plant diseases are caused by pathogens such as fungi, bacteria, and viruses, each with specific characteristics and modes of attack. By deepening your understanding of these pathogens, you can develop more effective strategies to prevent and manage diseases in your greenhouse.

Fungal Diseases

Fungi are the most common pathogens causing diseases in greenhouse environments. They thrive in moist, humid conditions and can spread rapidly. Common fungal diseases include:

- **Powdery Mildew**: Characterized by white powdery spots on leaves and stems, this disease can stunt plant growth and distort leaves.

- **Botrytis (Gray Mold)**: This fungus affects many plant species, especially in cool, moist conditions. It causes gray mold on flowers, leaves, and stems and can lead to significant crop loss.

- **Root Rots**: Caused by fungi like Phytophthora and Fusarium, root rots lead to the decay of root systems, resulting in wilted and stunted plants. Overwatering and poor drainage are common culprits.

Bacterial Diseases

Bacterial pathogens can also wreak havoc in greenhouses, often favored by warm, humid conditions. These diseases are typically harder to control once they establish within the plant population. Examples include:

- **Bacterial Leaf Spot**: Manifests as small, water-soaked spots on leaves that can enlarge and merge, causing significant leaf damage and drop.

- **Bacterial Wilt**: This disease causes plants to wilt and die rapidly without much warning. It blocks the water transport system in plants, leading to severe dehydration.

Viral Diseases

Viruses are microscopic organisms that require living cells to multiply. They are often transmitted by insects or through infected tools and hands. Viral diseases are difficult to treat and can lead to:

- **Mosaic Virus**: Symptoms include mottled green or yellow coloring on leaves, stunted growth, and malformed fruits.

- **Leaf Curl**: This virus causes leaves to curl and distort, often with a reduction in the overall growth rate of the plant.

Diagnosis and Identification

Proper diagnosis of plant diseases involves a combination of visual inspection, understanding of the plant's growing conditions, and sometimes laboratory analysis. Signs of plant diseases include:

- **Unusual leaf discolorations or patterns**
- **Wilting or drooping despite adequate water**
- **Spots or blisters on leaves or stems**
- **Rotten smells from the soil or plant base**
- **Sudden loss of leaves or flowers**

Integrated Management Strategies

Managing plant diseases effectively requires an integrated approach:

- **Cultural Controls**: Adjusting the greenhouse environment to make it less hospitable to pathogens. This includes optimizing air circulation, humidity levels, and temperature.

- **Physical Removal**: Regularly removing and destroying infected plant parts or entire plants to prevent the spread of disease.

- **Chemical Treatments**: Using fungicides, bactericides, and virucides judiciously when necessary and ensuring they are suitable for use in a greenhouse setting.

- **Biological Controls**: Introducing beneficial organisms that naturally combat pathogens, such as bacteria that inhibit fungal growth or predatory mites that reduce the population of virus-spreading insect vectors.

By deepening your understanding of these pathogens and their environmental preferences, you can tailor your greenhouse management practices to prevent outbreaks and respond swiftly and effectively when diseases occur. The goal is to maintain a balanced ecosystem where healthy plants can thrive with minimal interference from diseases.

Prevention Strategies

Preventing plant diseases in a greenhouse setting is crucial for maintaining a healthy and productive environment for your plants. Implementing effective prevention strategies can significantly reduce the risk of disease outbreaks, safeguarding your investment and labor. Here are some detailed strategies to help you keep your greenhouse disease-free:

Environmental Control

1. Optimize Air Circulation and Ventilation: Proper air circulation helps prevent the buildup of excess humidity and moisture on plant surfaces, conditions that are ideal for many pathogens. Ensure that your greenhouse has adequate ventilation systems in place, such as fans and vents that can be adjusted according to the weather conditions.

2. Manage Humidity Levels: Use dehumidifiers or increase ventilation during damp weather to keep humidity levels within a range that is unfavorable for disease development. The ideal humidity level often depends on the plants you are growing, but generally, keeping it below 50-60% can help minimize disease risks.

Cultural Practices

3. Sanitation: Regular cleaning and disinfection of greenhouse surfaces, tools, pots, and trays can prevent the spread of pathogens. Use a solution of bleach or commercial disinfectant to clean tools and surfaces regularly.

4. Remove Plant Debris: Promptly remove and properly dispose of plant debris and dead leaves, which can harbor fungi and other pathogens. This includes cleaning up leaf litter from the floor and ensuring that all organic waste is removed from the premises.

5. Soil and Substrate Management: Use sterile potting mixes to avoid introducing pathogens into the greenhouse. If reusing pots or trays, ensure they are thoroughly cleaned and disinfected before refilling them with new soil.

Plant Management

6. Select Disease-Resistant Varieties: Whenever possible, choose plant varieties that are known to be resistant to common diseases. These varieties have been bred to possess genetic resistance to certain pathogens, significantly reducing the need for chemical interventions.

7. Proper Plant Spacing: Overcrowding plants can create a microenvironment that is conducive to the development of diseases. Proper spacing allows for adequate air flow around each plant, reducing humidity and minimizing the risk of disease spread.

8. Quarantine New Plants: Always quarantine new plants before introducing them into your greenhouse to ensure they are not carrying pests or diseases. Keep them isolated in a separate area for a few weeks while monitoring them for any signs of illness.

Monitoring and Early Detection

9. Regular Monitoring: Regularly inspect your plants for signs of disease, such as spotting, wilting, or unusual growth patterns. Early detection is key to preventing the spread of disease within your greenhouse.

10. Implement a Scouting Schedule: Develop a routine schedule to inspect and monitor plant health, documenting any symptoms or irregularities. This can help you track the effectiveness of your prevention strategies and make timely decisions about interventions.

Integrated Pest Management (IPM)

11. Use Biological Controls: Integrate beneficial insects or microorganisms that combat or outcompete disease-causing pathogens. For example, introducing beneficial nematodes can control soil-borne fungal diseases.

12. Apply Organic Fungicides: As a preventive measure, you can apply organic fungicides that are less harmful to the environment and non-toxic to humans. Products containing copper and sulfur, as well as biofungicides that contain beneficial bacteria or fungi, can provide effective disease prevention.

Education and Training

13. Train Staff and Volunteers: If you work with a team, ensure that everyone is trained in disease recognition, sanitation practices, and the proper handling of plants. An educated team can be your first line of defense against plant diseases.

By integrating these strategies into your daily and seasonal greenhouse routines, you can create a robust system of prevention that minimizes the risk of plant diseases. Consistent application of these practices, combined with a proactive approach to garden management, will help ensure that your greenhouse remains a vibrant and productive environment.

Early detection and accurate diagnosis of plant diseases are pivotal in a greenhouse setting to ensure timely and effective management. By recognizing symptoms as soon as they appear, gardeners can take steps to contain and treat diseases before they become widespread, thereby safeguarding their plant investments. Below are detailed descriptions of common symptoms and effective organic treatment options:

Early Detection and Diagnosis

Symptom Identification:

- **Leaf Spots and Blights:** Look for irregular or circular spots that may be brown, black, or yellowish in color. These spots often signify fungal or bacterial infections.

- **Stunted Growth or Wilting:** This can indicate a range of issues, including root rot diseases caused by overwatering or a fungal infection in the root zone.

- **Discoloration or Deformation:** Yellowing leaves might suggest nutrient deficiencies or viral infections. Deformed growth, such as curled or twisted leaves, could be a sign of pest damage or viral diseases.

Monitoring Tools and Techniques:

- **Regular Scouting:** Walk through your greenhouse daily to inspect plants closely, using a magnifying glass if necessary to spot early signs of trouble.

- **Moisture Sensors and Climate Controls:** Implement tools that help maintain optimal growing conditions to prevent disease-friendly environments.

- **Photographic Documentation:** Keep a visual record of plant progress and symptoms for comparison over time or consultation with experts.

Organic Treatment Options

When diseases are detected, the following organic methods can be employed to manage and mitigate their effects:

1. Copper and Sulfur Sprays:

- **Usage:** These are broad-spectrum treatments effective against many fungal and bacterial diseases. Copper fungicides can be used to treat leaf spots, blights, and bacterial infections, while sulfur is particularly effective against powdery mildew.

- **Considerations:** Use these treatments sparingly and only as directed to minimize environmental impact and avoid harming beneficial soil organisms and insects.

2. Biological Controls:

- **Beneficial Microbes:** Bacillus subtilis and Trichoderma are examples of beneficial microbes that act as biofungicides. They work by outcompeting disease-causing pathogens for space and nutrients or by directly antagonizing them.

- **Application:** These can be applied via watering systems or as foliar sprays, depending on the product and the type of disease.

3. Botanical Extracts:

- **Neem Oil:** This natural oil is extracted from the neem tree and works by disrupting the life cycle of fungi and deterring insects. It's effective against rust, scab, and mildew.

- **Garlic and Chilli Sprays:** Homemade concoctions made from garlic or chilli can deter pests and reduce fungal growth due to their natural antimicrobial properties.

Implementing an Integrated Approach

Combining these methods into an integrated disease management strategy enhances effectiveness and sustainability:

- **Rotation of Treatments:** Rotate different types of organic treatments to prevent pathogens from developing resistance.

- **Companion Planting:** Grow plants together that can mutually benefit from each other's presence, reducing the likelihood of disease.

- **Enhance Biodiversity:** Increasing the variety of plants can help break disease cycles and improve the overall health of the greenhouse ecosystem.

By focusing on early detection and employing organic treatment strategies, greenhouse gardeners can effectively manage plant diseases while maintaining an environmentally friendly approach. This proactive stance not only preserves the health of the plants but also ensures that the greenhouse remains a safe, sustainable, and productive space.

Integrated Disease Management

Adopting an integrated approach to disease management in your greenhouse involves combining cultural, biological, and chemical methods to create a robust defense against diseases:

- **Crop Rotation**: Even in a greenhouse, rotating plants can prevent the buildup of soil-borne diseases and pests.

- **Diversity**: Plant a variety of species to reduce the risk of widespread disease outbreaks. Diverse plantings can interrupt the life cycle of many pathogens.

- **Monitoring**: Keep a regular schedule for inspecting plants, using sticky traps and other monitoring tools to check for early signs of disease.

Record Keeping

Maintain detailed records of all plants, noting any signs of disease, treatments applied, and their outcomes. This documentation will help you identify patterns and potentially problematic areas in your greenhouse, allowing for targeted adjustments to your management strategies.

Engaging with Expert Resources

Don't hesitate to consult with extension services, experienced greenhouse growers, or plant pathologists when faced with persistent or unidentified disease issues. Expert advice can be invaluable in diagnosing and managing complex plant health problems.

By employing these strategies, you not only protect your plants from diseases but also enhance your greenhouse's overall productivity and health. Remember, a healthy plant is less likely to succumb to diseases, so focus on creating and maintaining an optimal growing environment. With diligent care and attention, your greenhouse can continue to be a lush, productive haven year-round.

CHAPTER 10: SUSTAINABILITY PRACTICES IN GREENHOUSE GARDENING

10.1. ECO-FRIENDLY MATERIALS AND CONSTRUCTION

The Cornerstone of Greenhouses: Frames and Foundations

The structural integrity of a greenhouse hinges on its frame and foundation. Opting for eco-friendly materials can significantly reduce your environmental footprint while ensuring durability and functionality.

Frames:

- **Wood:** Choosing sustainably sourced wood, such as cedar or redwood, is beneficial due to its natural resistance to decay and insects. Ensure the wood is certified by the Forest Stewardship Council (FSC), which guarantees it comes from responsibly managed forests.

- **Bamboo:** An excellent alternative due to its rapid growth and minimal pesticide requirements. Bamboo frames provide a robust, lightweight, and renewable option, contributing to lower environmental impact and offering a unique aesthetic appeal.

- **Recycled Metal:** If metal is your preference, look for recycled aluminum or steel. These materials offer strength and longevity while reducing the need for new metal production, which is energy-intensive.

Foundations:

- **Rammed Earth:** This sustainable technique involves compacting a mixture of earth and a small amount of cement. Rammed earth foundations are not only environmentally friendly but also provide excellent thermal mass, helping to regulate temperature within the greenhouse.

- **Recycled Concrete or Bricks:** Utilizing recycled materials for the foundation reduces waste and the demand for new resources. These materials provide a solid base while contributing to sustainability goals.

The Envelope: Walls and Glazing

The walls and glazing of your greenhouse play a crucial role in light diffusion, insulation, and overall environmental impact.

Glazing:

- **Polycarbonate Panels:** These panels are durable, offer excellent light diffusion, and are often made from recycled materials. They are lighter than glass, reducing transportation energy, and more resistant to breakage.

- **Polyethylene Film:** Advanced polyethylene films with UV stabilizers and anti-dust properties can be recycled, providing an eco-friendly option for covering greenhouses.

- **Recycled Glass:** Though challenging to source and handle, recycled glass is an excellent option for those committed to sustainability. It offers superior light transmission and adds a vintage charm to the structure.

Insulation:

- **Straw Bales:** Providing high insulation value, straw bales are a renewable resource that can be used for insulating the lower parts of the greenhouse walls.

- **Sheep's Wool:** Naturally insulative and biodegradable, sheep's wool is an excellent choice for maintaining a stable internal temperature without the environmental cost of synthetic materials.

Nurturing Nature with Nature: Green Roofs and Living Walls

Green Roofs:

- **Benefits:** Green roofs offer insulation, reduce stormwater runoff, and provide a habitat for beneficial insects and birds. They also improve air quality and enhance the aesthetic appeal of your greenhouse.

- **Implementation:** Choose lightweight, drought-resistant plants suited to your local climate. Ensure the greenhouse structure can support the additional weight and that the roof is adequately waterproofed.

Living Walls:

- **Benefits:** Living walls or vertical gardens provide similar benefits to green roofs, such as improved insulation and biodiversity. They can also maximize space within the greenhouse for growing a variety of plants.

- **Implementation:** Use modular systems or create your own vertical planters using recycled materials. Incorporate an efficient irrigation system to maintain plant health.

The Foundation of Sustainability: Water Management

Water is a critical resource in greenhouse gardening, and managing it sustainably is essential.

Rainwater Harvesting:

- **Systems:** Install gutters and downspouts to collect rainwater, storing it in barrels or tanks for later use. This reduces reliance on municipal water supplies and conserves a valuable resource.

- **Solar-Powered Pumps:** Utilize solar energy to power water pumps for irrigation, further reducing the greenhouse's carbon footprint.

Graywater Systems:

- **Reuse:** Recycle household water from sinks, showers, and washing machines for irrigation. Ensure the graywater is free from harmful chemicals and suitable for plant use.

The Art of Assembly: Sustainable Construction Methods

Prefabrication:

- **Benefits:** Prefabricated parts minimize on-site waste and streamline construction. Choose kits that use sustainable materials to enhance efficiency and reduce environmental impact.

Tool Use:

- **Manual and Electric Tools:** Opt for manual tools or electric tools powered by renewable energy sources to minimize greenhouse gas emissions during construction.

Embracing the Old: Repurposing and Upcycling

Creative Use of Recycled Materials:

- **Windows and Doors:** Repurpose old windows and doors to build the greenhouse structure. This practice not only reduces waste but also adds character and uniqueness to the greenhouse.

A Lifetime of Learning: Educate and Engage

Community Involvement:

- **Workshops and Tours:** Host events to educate others about eco-friendly greenhouse construction and share your experiences. Engaging with the community fosters a culture of sustainability and spreads knowledge about environmentally responsible gardening practices.

Building a greenhouse with eco-friendly materials and sustainable construction methods is a commitment to both your garden and the planet. By carefully selecting materials, employing innovative techniques, and continuously educating yourself and others, you create a thriving, sustainable greenhouse that serves as a model for environmental stewardship. Your efforts not only yield a bountiful harvest but also contribute to a healthier, greener world for future generations.

10.2. WATER CONSERVATION TECHNIQUES

Collecting and Using Rainwater

Harnessing rainwater for greenhouse irrigation is one of the simplest and most effective ways to conserve water. By installing gutters and downspouts along the roof of your greenhouse, you can channel rainwater into storage barrels or cisterns. This practice not only reduces dependence on municipal water supplies but also provides plants with naturally soft water free from chlorine and other chemicals typically found in tap water.

Steps to Implement Rainwater Harvesting:

1. **Install Gutters and Downspouts:** Attach gutters along the roof edges to collect rainwater. Ensure they lead to downspouts directing water into storage containers.

2. **Choose Storage Containers:** Select barrels or cisterns that are large enough to store adequate amounts of water for your greenhouse needs. Ensure they have lids to prevent debris and mosquito breeding.

3. **Connect to Irrigation Systems:** Attach a hose or drip irrigation system to the storage containers to efficiently distribute the collected water to your plants.

Watering Wisely

The timing and method of watering can significantly influence water conservation. Early morning is the optimal time to water plants because cooler temperatures reduce evaporation, allowing plants to absorb more moisture. Avoid watering in the evening as it can lead to high humidity levels overnight, promoting diseases.

Efficient Watering Techniques:

- **Drip Irrigation:** Drip systems deliver water directly to the plant roots, minimizing evaporation and runoff. These systems can be automated and equipped with moisture sensors to provide precise watering.

- **Soaker Hoses:** Similar to drip irrigation, soaker hoses release water slowly along their length, providing consistent moisture directly to the soil.

- **Hand Watering:** For smaller greenhouses, hand watering with a watering can or hose fitted with a water breaker nozzle can be effective. This method allows for targeted watering and reduces wastage.

Recycling Water Within the Ecosystem

Embracing a closed-loop system such as aquaponics can maximize water use efficiency in your greenhouse. Aquaponics combines fish farming with hydroponic plant cultivation, creating a symbiotic environment where fish waste provides natural nutrients for the plants, and plants filter the water for the fish.

Benefits of Aquaponics:

- **Water Efficiency:** Water is continually recirculated in the system, drastically reducing the amount needed compared to traditional gardening methods.

- **Nutrient-Rich Water:** Fish waste supplies plants with essential nutrients, reducing the need for additional fertilizers.

- **Sustainable Practice:** Aquaponics creates a self-sustaining ecosystem, promoting biodiversity and reducing resource consumption.

Soil Management and Mulching

Healthy soil with high organic matter content can retain water more effectively, reducing the need for frequent watering. Incorporating compost and other organic materials into your soil improves its water-holding capacity.

Mulching Techniques:

- **Organic Mulches:** Materials like straw, wood chips, or leaf mold help retain soil moisture, suppress weeds, and reduce temperature fluctuations.

- **Inorganic Mulches:** Gravel or plastic mulches can also be effective in conserving moisture, though they may not provide the added benefits of organic mulches.

Plant Choices and Placement

Selecting drought-tolerant plants and strategically placing them can significantly reduce water use. Grouping plants with similar water requirements allows for more targeted watering, minimizing waste.

Drought-Tolerant Plants:

- **Succulents:** These plants store water in their leaves and require minimal watering.

- **Herbs:** Many herbs, such as rosemary and thyme, thrive in drier conditions and are well-suited for water-efficient gardening.

Frequent Monitoring and Maintenance

Regularly inspecting your greenhouse for water usage efficiency is crucial. Check for leaks in irrigation systems, ensure proper drainage, and adjust watering schedules based on plant needs and weather conditions.

Monitoring Tools:

- **Moisture Meters:** These tools help determine soil moisture levels, ensuring you only water when necessary.

- **Timers and Sensors:** Automated systems with timers and moisture sensors can optimize watering schedules and reduce water waste.

Eco-Friendly Practices and Education

Educating yourself and engaging with the gardening community on water conservation techniques fosters a culture of sustainability. Share your knowledge through workshops, tours, and discussions to inspire others to adopt eco-friendly practices.

Community Engagement:

- **Workshops:** Host events to demonstrate rainwater harvesting, drip irrigation, and other water-saving techniques.

- **Online Platforms:** Share your experiences and tips on social media or gardening forums to reach a broader audience.

Conclusion

Water conservation in greenhouse gardening is a holistic practice that integrates efficient watering methods, rainwater harvesting, soil management, and sustainable plant choices. By adopting these techniques, you not only ensure the health and vitality of your plants but also contribute to a more sustainable and eco-friendly gardening approach. Each drop saved is a step towards a greener future, reflecting your commitment to both your garden and the planet.

10.3. ORGANIC GARDENING AND COMPOSTING

Organic Gardening: Cultivating Harmony

Organic gardening is more than just a method—it's a holistic approach that seeks to work with nature rather than against it. By eliminating synthetic chemicals and embracing natural processes, you create a balanced ecosystem that fosters healthy plants and soil.

The Virtues of Going Organic

Choosing organic gardening brings numerous benefits:

- **Healthier Plants**: Organic fertilizers and natural pest control methods strengthen plant resilience, leading to healthier growth.

- **Improved Biodiversity**: Encouraging diverse plant species and beneficial insects promotes a balanced ecosystem.

- **Personal and Environmental Health**: Reducing chemical use protects your health and the surrounding environment.

- **Enhanced Taste and Nutrition**: Many gardeners believe that organic produce tastes better and may have higher nutritional value.

- **Sustainability**: Organic practices reduce reliance on non-renewable resources and enhance soil health.

Composting: The Circle of Life

Composting is the natural process of recycling organic matter into nutrient-rich soil. This sustainable practice transforms kitchen scraps, garden waste, and other organic materials into compost, a valuable resource for your greenhouse garden.

Benefits of Composting

Composting offers several advantages:

- **Improves Soil Structure**: Compost enhances soil texture, making it easier for plant roots to penetrate and grow.

- **Increases Water Retention**: Compost helps soil retain moisture, reducing the need for frequent watering.

- **Provides Nutrients**: Compost acts as a slow-release fertilizer, providing essential nutrients over time.

- **Suppresses Diseases**: Healthy compost can help suppress soil-borne diseases and pests.

Organic Gardening in Practice

Soil Management

Healthy soil is the foundation of organic gardening. Incorporate compost and organic fertilizers, such as worm castings or fish emulsion, to enrich the soil. These natural amendments improve soil fertility and structure.

Crop Rotation

Practice crop rotation in your greenhouse to prevent nutrient depletion and reduce the buildup of pests and diseases. Rotate plant families to different areas each growing season to maintain soil health and minimize pest problems.

Companion Planting

Planting certain species together can naturally repel pests and improve growth. For example, planting basil near tomatoes can deter pests like aphids and enhance tomato flavor.

Cultivating a Compost Ecosystem

Starting Your Compost

Begin with a simple compost bin or designated area for composting. Balance green materials (rich in nitrogen, such as vegetable scraps and grass clippings) with brown materials (rich in carbon, such as dried leaves and straw).

Maintaining Your Compost

Turn your compost regularly to aerate it and speed up decomposition. Keep the compost moist, but not waterlogged, and ensure it receives adequate airflow. Over time, the materials will break down into dark, nutrient-rich compost.

Mindful Choices for a Healthy Greenhouse

Choosing Plants

Select plant varieties that are well-suited to your greenhouse conditions and resistant to common pests and diseases. Use organic seeds and transplants to ensure your garden remains free of synthetic chemicals from the start.

Natural Pest Control

Embrace natural pest control methods, such as introducing beneficial insects like ladybugs and lacewings. These predators help control pest populations without harmful chemicals.

Efficient Watering

Implement water-saving techniques like drip irrigation to minimize water waste and ensure plants receive consistent moisture directly at their roots.

The Path to a Sustainable Future

Adopting organic gardening and composting practices in your greenhouse is a step towards a sustainable future. By nurturing your plants and soil with natural methods, you contribute to a healthier environment and promote biodiversity.

Community Engagement

Share your organic gardening and composting practices with your community. Host workshops, give tours, or participate in gardening forums to inspire others to adopt sustainable practices.

Continuous Learning

Stay informed about new organic gardening techniques and innovations. The field is always evolving, and continuous learning helps you improve your practices and yield better results.

By committing to organic gardening and composting, you play a crucial role in fostering a sustainable environment. Your greenhouse becomes more than a place to grow plants—it becomes a testament to your dedication to preserving the earth's resources and promoting ecological balance. As you nurture your garden, remember that each organic choice you make contributes to a healthier planet for future generations.

CHAPTER 11: EXTENDING YOUR GREENHOUSE USE

Understanding the Greenhouse Environment

Gardening year-round in a greenhouse requires a deep understanding of the greenhouse environment. This enclosed space allows you to control temperature, humidity, and light, creating ideal conditions for plant growth regardless of external weather conditions. Here are some key factors to consider:

Temperature Control

- **Winter Heating**: Maintain a consistent temperature using heaters, thermal mass (like water barrels or stone), and proper insulation. Aim to keep the temperature above freezing for cool-season crops and warmer for heat-loving plants.

- **Summer Cooling**: Prevent overheating with shade cloths, ventilations such as roof vents and side vents, and possibly evaporative cooling systems.

Light Management

- **Supplemental Lighting**: Use LED grow lights to extend daylight hours during shorter days, ensuring plants receive adequate light for photosynthesis and growth.

- **Light Intensity**: Adjust the distance of lights to maintain optimal light intensity, preventing plants from becoming leggy or stressed.

Humidity and Ventilation

- **Humidity Control**: Use fans and dehumidifiers to maintain optimal humidity levels, preventing fungal diseases and promoting healthy plant growth.

- **Air Circulation**: Ensure proper air circulation to reduce the risk of mold and mildew. Oscillating fans can help evenly distribute air.

Seasonal Adaptations

Each season brings unique challenges and opportunities for greenhouse gardening. Adapting your practices to these seasonal changes is essential for successful year-round gardening.

Winter

- **Cool-Season Crops**: Focus on growing hardy greens like spinach, kale, and root vegetables such as carrots and beets.

- **Insulation**: Add extra layers of insulation, such as bubble wrap or thermal blankets, to retain heat.

- **Minimal Watering**: Reduce watering frequency to prevent excess humidity and root rot.

Spring

- **Seed Starting**: Begin seedlings early for summer crops, utilizing the warming temperatures to give them a head start.

- **Ventilation**: Gradually increase ventilation to accommodate the warming weather and prevent overheating.

- **Transplanting**: Move hardy seedlings to their final positions once temperatures stabilize.

Summer

- **Heat-Loving Crops**: Grow tomatoes, peppers, cucumbers, and other warm-season crops.

- **Shade Management**: Use shade cloths to protect plants from intense sunlight and prevent heat stress.

- **Frequent Watering**: Increase watering frequency to match the higher evaporation rates and plant water needs.

Autumn

- **Succession Planting**: Plant cool-season crops for a continuous harvest as summer crops finish.

- **Temperature Monitoring**: Prepare for fluctuating temperatures by adjusting ventilation and heating as needed.

- **Cleanup and Sanitation**: Remove spent plants and clean the greenhouse to prevent pest and disease carryover.

Crop Selection and Techniques

Choosing the right plants and employing effective growing techniques are crucial for maximizing greenhouse productivity.

Crop Selection

- **Cool-Season Crops**: Lettuce, spinach, kale, radishes, carrots, and beets thrive in cooler temperatures.

- **Warm-Season Crops**: Tomatoes, peppers, cucumbers, and melons flourish in warmer conditions with adequate light.

- **Perennial Crops**: Herbs like rosemary, mint, and thyme, as well as fruits like strawberries and figs, can be grown year-round with proper care.

Growing Techniques

- **Vertical Gardening**: Utilize vertical space with trellises, hanging pots, and stacked planters to maximize limited ground area.

- **Succession Planting**: Stagger planting times to ensure a continuous harvest throughout the year.

- **Intercropping**: Grow quick-maturing crops alongside slower-growing ones to maximize space and reduce pest pressure.

- **Crop Rotation**: Rotate crops within the greenhouse to prevent soil nutrient depletion and reduce pest and disease buildup.

Watering Strategies

Proper watering is critical to maintaining healthy plants and preventing diseases.

Drip Irrigation

- **Efficient Water Use**: Drip irrigation delivers water directly to the roots, minimizing evaporation and runoff.

- **Automated Systems**: Use timers and moisture sensors to automate watering, ensuring plants receive consistent moisture.

Mulching

- **Moisture Retention**: Apply organic mulch to soil surfaces to retain moisture and reduce the frequency of watering.

- **Weed Suppression**: Mulch also helps suppress weed growth, reducing competition for water and nutrients.

Record Keeping and Community Engagement

Maintaining detailed records and engaging with the gardening community can enhance your greenhouse gardening success.

Record Keeping

- **Track Data**: Record temperature, humidity, watering schedules, plant growth, and harvest dates to identify patterns and improve practices.

- **Analyze Results**: Use your data to make informed decisions about crop selection, planting times, and environmental adjustments.

Community Engagement

- **Share Knowledge**: Participate in gardening forums, social media groups, and local gardening clubs to share experiences and learn from others.

- **Workshops and Tours**: Host workshops or greenhouse tours to educate others about year-round gardening and sustainable practices.

Flexibility and Adaptation

The key to successful year-round gardening is flexibility and adaptation. Conditions will vary, and unexpected challenges will arise. By remaining observant and willing to adjust your practices, you can create a thriving greenhouse garden that produces fresh produce throughout the year.

Embrace the continuous learning process, celebrate your successes, and view setbacks as opportunities for growth. Your greenhouse is not just a place for plants to grow; it's a space for you to cultivate your skills, knowledge, and connection to nature. Through thoughtful planning, diligent care, and a commitment to sustainability, you can enjoy the fruits of your labor in every season, making your greenhouse a year-round haven of productivity and beauty.

11.2. ADVANCED TECHNIQUES: GRAFTING AND CLONING

Grafting: Union of Vigor and Variety

Grafting is an ancient horticultural technique that involves joining two plant parts to grow as one. The part providing the root system is called the "rootstock," while the part providing the desired stems, leaves, flowers, or fruit is called the "scion." This technique allows gardeners to combine the strengths of different plants, producing specimens that offer the disease resistance of one plant with the fruiting prowess of another.

The Why and When of Grafting

Grafting can significantly enhance your gardening efforts by enabling you to:

- **Overcome Soil-Borne Diseases**: Use a rootstock that is resistant to diseases affecting sensitive varieties.

- **Hasten Plant Maturity**: Enjoy blooms or fruits more quickly than from seed-grown plants.

- **Save Failing Plants**: Preserve a cherished variety by grafting its healthy parts onto a robust rootstock.

Grafting is best done in late winter or early spring when plants begin to emerge from dormancy and sap starts to flow. However, some grafting techniques work well during summer when both the rootstock and scion are actively growing.

The Grafting Process

1. **Select Healthy Rootstock**: Choose a rootstock free from pests and diseases with a robust root system.

2. **Choose a Desirable Scion**: Pick a scion from a variety known for good production or other desirable traits. The scion should be about the thickness of a pencil and have several buds.

3. **Make Clean Cuts**: Depending on the grafting method, make sloping cuts, a V-shape, or a budding cut on both the rootstock and scion.

4. **Join the Scion to the Rootstock**: Align the cambium layers (the growth tissue beneath the bark) of both pieces for a successful graft.

5. **Secure the Union**: Use grafting tape or a similar material to secure the graft, and seal the wound with a grafting compound to prevent desiccation and disease.

Monitor the grafted plant for support and remove any sprouts that emerge below the graft to ensure all energy goes into developing the grafted variety.

Cloning: A Copy-Paste in Horticulture

Cloning, also known as vegetative propagation, involves taking cuttings from a "mother plant" and encouraging them to form new roots. This method creates exact genetic replicas, making it invaluable for reproducing plants with specific desired traits.

Why Clone?

Cloning is beneficial because it:

- **Guarantees Uniformity**: Each clone is a genetic duplicate of the parent plant.

- **Saves Space**: Eliminates the need to grow from seed to identify desirable traits.

- **Speeds Up Production**: Clones can reach maturity faster than seedlings.

The Art of Cloning

1. **Select the Mother Plant**: Choose a vigorous, healthy plant that has not yet flowered.

2. **Prepare Tools**: Use sterilized pruning shears or blades to prevent disease transmission.

3. **Take Cuttings**: Cut a segment about 4-6 inches long, ideally just below a leaf node, at a 45-degree angle to increase the rooting surface area.

4. **Remove Lower Leaves**: Strip leaves from the lower half of the cutting to expose nodes for root development.

5. **Apply Rooting Hormone**: Dip the cutting end into rooting hormone to encourage root growth.

6. **Insert into Growing Medium**: Place the cutting into a medium designed for rooting, such as peat moss, perlite, or rooting cubes.

7. **Maintain Humidity**: Use a humidity dome or plastic covering to keep the environment moist but not waterlogged.

8. **Monitor for Root Development**: Check for root growth over a few weeks. Once roots form and the plant shows new growth, it's ready to be transplanted.

Enhancing Your Greenhouse with Advanced Techniques

Mastering grafting and cloning can significantly enhance the productivity and diversity of your greenhouse. These techniques are not just practical methods but are also steeped in horticultural tradition, reflecting a deep connection with the natural world.

Grafting and Cloning Best Practices

- **Stay Patient**: Both grafting and cloning require patience and practice. Expect some failures initially as you learn the nuances of each technique.

- **Record Your Successes and Failures**: Keeping detailed notes on your grafting and cloning attempts will help you refine your methods and increase your success rates over time.

- **Share Knowledge**: Engaging with other gardeners, either locally or online, can provide valuable insights and support.

Embracing the Tradition and Innovation

By integrating grafting and cloning into your greenhouse practices, you're not just expanding your gardening skills—you're embracing a rich horticultural heritage. These techniques offer a bridge between traditional gardening wisdom and modern innovation, enhancing your ability to cultivate a diverse and productive greenhouse.

Conclusion

Advanced techniques like grafting and cloning open up a world of possibilities for greenhouse gardening. They enable you to produce stronger, more diverse plants, and ensure that your garden is not only a source of beauty and sustenance but also a testament to your dedication and skill as a gardener. By mastering these techniques, you become a more resilient and innovative cultivator, capable of creating a thriving greenhouse ecosystem year-round.

Community Engagement and Sharing Your Harvest

The art of greenhouse gardening opens up a world of possibility not just for personal gain but for a flourishing community connection. Sharing the fruits of your labor can be one of the most rewarding aspects of cultivating plants in your personal oasis, creating bonds with neighbors and friends through the universal language of fresh produce. Here, we explore the multifaceted benefits of community engagement and the gratifying experience of sharing your harvest.

The Ripple Effect of Sharing Your Greenhouse Bounty

Imagine this: a crisp morning in your lush greenhouse, the air buzzing with the tender sounds of nature. In your hands, you hold a basket of freshly picked vegetables, vibrant and bursting with life. But this richness is not just for you. By sharing your harvest, you contribute to a wave of positive change that extends far beyond your garden doors.

Growing for Others: Greenhouse gardening affords you a surplus that can be the cornerstone of community sharing. Planting with the intent to distribute to others can reshape the way you approach your harvesting calendar. Rather than solely focusing on what you and your family consume, consider crops that are in

115

demand locally, whether they're staples like tomatoes and cucumbers or more diverse, culturally specific varieties that resonate with your community's palette. This practice not only diversifies your gardening skills but also fosters an inclusive community spirit.

Creating Connections and Fostering Goodwill: Sharing the yield from your greenhouse is a natural icebreaker and a catalyst for building profound connections with those around you. Each tomato, pepper, or herb bundle becomes a token of goodwill, a way to strengthen existing relationships and kindle new ones. This communal exchange promotes a sense of belonging and cultivates a network of individuals who value sustainability and self-sufficiency.

Education and Inspiration: When you open up your greenhouse to visitors or distribute harvests, every interaction is an opportunity to educate others about the importance of sustainable practices and the tangible benefits of home gardening. Your greenhouse becomes an informal classroom where knowledge about plant cultivation flourishes. As your neighbors learn about the meticulous care that goes into each plant, they grow to appreciate the value of locally-grown, pesticide-free produce, potentially inspiring them to start their own green thumb journey.

Sharing Your Harvest: A Practical How-To

So, how can you best share your greenhouse harvest with your community? Let's walk through a few practical avenues.

Community Giving: Whether it's through local food banks, church groups, or school programs, donating your surplus produce is a meaningful way to contribute to the community's overall well-being. Contact organizations in advance to understand their needs and any guidelines they might have. Timing, packaging, and even the type of crops accepted can be crucial for a successful donation.

Start a Greenhouse Club: A greenhouse club in your area can do wonders. It can be an open-door policy for like-minded friends to share tips, seeds, and surplus. Not only does this allow for trading fruits and vegetables, but it also facilitates the swapping of experiences, advice on pest management, and creative gardening techniques.

Neighborhood Harvest Swap: Organize a casual neighborhood swap meet where everyone brings their homegrown produce to exchange. This kind of event can spin into regular gatherings, potlucks, or even seasonal fairs, creating a local tradition that celebrates the diversity of homegrown goods and nurtures community togetherness.

Seed Sharing: Part of the abundance lies in the seeds, the starters of future growth. Offering seeds from your plants to others is a powerful gesture, symbolizing trust and mutual support. It encourages biodiversity and helps preserve heirloom species that might otherwise get overlooked in commercial gardening.

Gardening Workshops: If you have mastered certain aspects of greenhouse gardening, consider holding workshops or teaching sessions. There's an undeniable charm in the hands-on approach, where participants can learn about potting, pruning, or even the basics of getting a greenhouse started. Your knowledge can empower others to initiate their sustainable journey.

Harvesting More Than Just Produce

The societal implications of sharing your greenhouse harvest resonate on a deeper level. By promoting self-sustaining agricultural practices within your local sphere, you contribute to food security and advocate for a more resilient community framework. You're not merely handing out fresh food; you're planting seeds of change that can lead to reduced food miles, lesser dependence on commercial farming, and a renewed appreciation for home-grown nutrition.

Remember that the ripple effect of community-bound greenhouse gardening is not solely about the quantity of produce shared but the quality of relationships and shared learning. The goal is not just to feed bodies but to nourish minds and hearts as well.

In Summary

Extending the usage of your greenhouse via community engagement and sharing your harvest transcends the mere act of growing food. It builds connections, fosters a sense of collective ownership over local food sources, and carves out spaces where individuals can learn, teach, and flourish together. Through each shared vegetable, each gardening workshop, and each swapped seedling, you're not just cultivating plants; you're nurturing a healthier, more connected, and sustainable future for all.